Everyday Grilling

Everyday Grilling

50 Recipes from Appetizers to Desserts

Sur La Table

**Andrews McMeel
Publishing, LLC**
Kansas City • Sydney • London

11 12 13 14 15 WKT 10 9 8 7 6 5 4 3 2 1

ISBN: 978-1-4494-0058-3

Library of Congress Control Number: 2010930544

Recipes adapted from *Things Cooks Love* and *Eating Local*

Photography: Ben Fink: p. 55; Gabe Hopkins: p. ii, ix, xvii, 2, 5, 6, 8, 22, 28, 46, 51, 83, 84, 93, 97, 101, 104, 109, 112; JohnsonRauhoff: p. vi, xi, xix, 15, 25, 45, 49, 53, 67, 91, 95; Sara Remington: p. 11, 18, 32, 37, 40, 58, 62, 65, 69, 70, 72, 73, 79, 89, 116;

Design: Holly Ogden

www.andrewsmcmeel.com
www.surlatable.com

• •

ATTENTION: SCHOOLS AND BUSINESSES
Andrews McMeel books are available at quantity discounts with bulk purchase for educational, business, or sales promotional use. For information, please write to: Special Sales Department, Andrews McMeel Publishing, LLC, 1130 Walnut Street, Kansas City, Missouri 64106.

Everyday Grilling

When annual grilling surveys ask people why they sear and sizzle foods outdoors, the most common answer is *flavor*. When foods are cooked over flame, the natural sugars caramelize, producing that delicious taste you get only from grilling. Grilled foods also look wonderful in an unmistakably rustic way—a little char, a few grill marks, and even the plainest chicken breast suddenly appears more tempting. Grilling outside also frees up the indoor kitchen and keeps mess to a minimum. And lastly, it's a cooking method that both men and women enjoy—every day, all throughout the year.

Everyday Grilling shows how to grill everything from appetizers to dessert. With today's easy-to-use grilling equipment, it's just as simple to grill or plank as it is to bake, roast, or broil. And you'll find a signature method, technique or recipe to make the most of local or regional foods for your whole meal throughout the seasons.

Getting Ready to Grill

Grilling is generally hot and fast, accomplished over direct heat (350° to 500°F). Boneless meats, fish fillets, and vegetables are all delicious cooked this way. But there are also special ways to grill bone-in meats, whole fish, game, cheese, and fruit, involving an indirect fire, a kiss of smoke, planking, stir-grilling, and other techniques.

And that involves decisions. What type of equipment? How hot a fire? How far away to place the food from the heat? Close the grill or keep it open? Smolder wood for extra flavor? Use a plank or a cast-iron griddle? Grill and baste foods on a spit? Most of these answers will be given in the recipes, but over time you may want to experiment and try variations on the given techniques.

From using skewers to a grill wok or a plank, from getting more flavor from wood chips or achieving a "black and blue" steak, there's a unique way to grill most foods. The right tool can make all the difference at the grill. Because they'll be used outdoors and in contact with heat and smoke, utensils that are heavier, of superior quality, and very durable make the best choice. Oiling utensils—and the grill grate—before using will help keep foods from sticking. Here are the basic tools to consider.

The Griller's Toolbox

Charcoal Chimneys or **Electric Fire Starters:** These are great for starting charcoal fires.

Stiff Wire Brush: Using a brush with a scraper makes cleaning the grill a simple job (tackle this while the grill is still warm).

Natural-Bristle Basting Brush: These are good for applying oil to the grill grates (before firing up the grill) and a separate brush to baste food during grilling or smoking.

Perforated Grill Racks: These are metal grates placed on top of the grill to keep small or delicate items, such as chicken wings, fish fillets, scallops, shrimp, and vegetables, from falling through the grill grates while cooking. Oil these before using.

Hinged Grill Baskets: These hold foods like fish steaks or whole fish, burgers, or asparagus in place and make turning easy.

Heat-Resistant Oven or **Grill Mitts:** These offer the best hand protection.

Long-Handled Spring-Loaded Tongs: These are easier to use than the scissors type. They are great for turning most food and skewers.

Spray Bottle: Filled with water will douse any flare-ups.

Long-Handled Offset Fish Spatula: One of these with a 5- to 6-inch blade makes for easy turning of fish fillets.

Instant-Read Thermometers: These offer a quick check for doneness when grilling meat and poultry.

Metal Smoker Boxes: These are very useful for holding wood chips that are placed over a gas grill fire to create smoke and hold in the flavor. Their perforations allow smoke to escape but keep chips from falling out.

Cooking on Charcoal Grills

Before lighting the grill, it should be clean. The grill rack(s) should be removed and lightly oiled with vegetable oil or wiped down with grill wipes.

A charcoal fire can be started in two safe, ecologically sound ways. The most chemical-free way is to use a charcoal chimney and hardwood charcoal and/or briquets. Hardwood charcoal, usually mesquite, is irregular in shape and burns hot and fast. Briquets are pressed into regular shapes and don't burn quite as hot. Many charcoal grillers use a combination of both.

The charcoal chimney is like a large metal coffee can with a handle. The top of the chimney is filled with hardwood lump charcoal and/or briquets. The chimney is then placed on a nonflammable surface, such as concrete or the grill rack. One to two sheets of crumpled newspaper are stuffed into the convex-shaped bottom. Then the newspaper is lit with the match of a long-handled lighter. After five minutes, the fire should still be going. If not, the process is repeated. The coals should be red-hot and starting to ash over in fifteen to twenty minutes. The hot coals are then carefully dumped into the bottom of the grill.

To use an electric fire starter, the charcoal is mounded on the bottom of the grill and the electric fire starter replaced on top, then plugged in. The coals will take about fifteen minutes to ignite. The starter is then carefully removed and set in a safe place to cool.

Direct Fire

When the charcoal is red-hot and beginning to ash over is the time to replace the oiled grill grate. The food is then placed on the grill grate directly over the hot coals. The grill lid can be open or closed, depending on the recipe. Any additional coals, for grill-roasting a chicken or anything that takes longer than forty-five minutes to cook, need to be ignited in the charcoal chimney before adding to the grill.

Herb grilling: Branches of fresh, woody herbs like rosemary, thyme, bay, or lavender are placed directly on the hot coals, with the grill closed to capture the aroma in the food. Alternatively, herb branches can also be placed on the grill grate or in a grill basket, then place the food on top of the herb branches. The herbs will smolder and sizzle, imparting flavor to your food, but the food will not have grill marks. Herb grilling is best with chicken, lamb, fish, or shellfish.

Stone griddle or Italian piastra grilling: A large stone or stone griddle is placed on the grill grate over direct heat to get very, very hot—so a drop of water will sizzle and evaporate almost immediately. Foods grill directly on the stone. Foods won't get grill marks, but will get scorch and sear marks over the very even heat. This technique works well with lamb, fish, steaks, or shellfish (with the grill lid down). The food is oiled, not the stone or griddle.

Cast-iron grilling: Similar to hot stone, but with a cast-iron skillet or griddle over direct heat. Again, the cast iron needs to get very, very hot so that it has a grayish cast. This technique works well with lamb, fish, or shellfish (with the grill lid down), and it gives steaks a real steakhouse flavor—without grill marks. The food is oiled, not the skillet.

Indirect Fire

A direct fire is prepared first. When the hot coals are in the bottom of the grill, the coals are pushed over to one side with a grill spatula or banked on both sides with a bare space in the center. The space that does not have hot coals is the indirect heat cooking side.

Wood-grilling: An indirect fire is prepared, as above. Water-soaked wood chips (for wood smoke flavoring) are placed on top of the coals. The grill grate is replaced, with the food placed on the indirect side. The grill lid is closed.

A World of Wood-Grilled Flavors: Natural hardwood chips can infuse foods with great smoke flavor while grilling on either a charcoal or gas grill.

Alder gives a light, aromatic flavor that's perfect with seafood.

Apple provides a sweeter, aromatic flavor that is good with poultry or pork.

Cherry lends a deeper, sweeter note to beef tenderloin, pork, poultry, or lamb.

Hickory gives a stronger, hearty smoke flavor to beef, pork, or poultry.

Mesquite provides the strongest, smokiest flavor and is well suited to beef.

Oak provides a medium smoke flavor without being bitter.

Pecan creates a medium smoke flavor, milder than hickory but stronger than oak.

Indirect herb grilling: Fresh herb branches are placed on top of the coals. The grill grate is replaced, with the food placed on the indirect side. The grill lid is closed.

Grill-roasting: Indirect grilling at approximately 350° to 400°F. The temperature is gauged by using a grill thermometer or by using the hand method described on page xiii. Food is placed on the indirect side. With the lid closed, the grill functions like an oven, only with more flavor!

Cooking on Gas Grills

Follow the manufacturer's directions for starting a gas grill. This will include attaching the propane tank to the grill, turning on the propane valve, then lighting the burners of the gas grill. About 40,000 combined BTUs (British Thermal Units, which measure the maximum heat output of a burner) are optimum for hot and fast grilling. Many grills have thermometers attached to the grill lid; closing the lid will allow the grill to heat up and the thermometer to correctly gauge the temperature.

Direct Fire

The burners are turned on. The food is placed on the grill grate directly over the hot burner, which is direct heat. To cook this way, the grill lid can be up or down.

Infrared grilling: This gas grill technology adds extra cooking power through infrared rays so food cooks even faster. The infrared switch is simply turned on. Because this results in increased heat, grilling is done with the lid up.

Herb grilling: Because debris from smoldering material can clog the gas jets, herb branches are placed in an aluminum foil packet with holes punched in it or in a metal smoker box. The packet or box is placed on the grill grate in a hot spot so the herbs will smolder safely. The grill is closed to capture the aroma in the food. Herb grilling is best with chicken, lamb, fish, or shellfish.

Stone griddle or Italian piastra grilling: A large stone or stone griddle is placed on the grill grate over direct heat to get very, very hot—so a drop of water will sizzle and evaporate almost immediately. Foods grill directly on the stone. Foods won't get grill marks but will display scorch and sear marks over the very even heat. This technique works well with lamb, fish, steaks, or shellfish (with the grill lid down). The food is oiled, not the stone or griddle.

Cast-iron grilling: Similar to hot stone, but with a cast-iron skillet or griddle over direct heat. Again, the cast iron needs to get very, very hot so it has a grayish cast. This technique works well with lamb, fish, or shellfish (with the grill lid down), and it gives steaks a real steakhouse flavor—without grill marks. The food is oiled, not the skillet.

Indirect Fire

The burners are lit on one half of the grill only. The side of the grill without the burners on is the indirect heat side. To cook this way, the grill lid must be closed.

Wood-grilling: Because debris from smoldering material can clog the gas jets, wood chips are placed in an aluminum foil packet with holes punched in it or in a metal smoker box. The packet or box is placed on the grill grate in a hot spot so the wood will smolder safely. The grill is closed to capture the smoky aroma in the food. See page xi for a list of the different wood-grilled flavors each type of chip produces.

How to Grill

When ready to grill, place the food over the hot fire. Grill food for half the cooking time on one side, allowing for good searing and grill marks. Turn once and finish cooking.

Grill Temperature

For a grill without a built-in thermometer, the hand method can be used.

If a hand can only be held 5 inches above the heat source for:

2 seconds, the fire is hot (450° to 500°F or more)

3 seconds, the fire is medium-hot (about 400°F)

4 seconds, the fire is medium (about 350°F)

On a charcoal grill, the temperature is lowered by slightly closing the side vents or by closing the lid, which deprives the fire of air. If the vents and the lid are both closed at the same time, the fire will go out. The temperature can be raised by opening the side vents or by adding more charcoal to the fire.

On a gas grill, the heat is adjusted by turning the heat control knobs to the desired level. The temperature can be increased by closing the lid or lowered by keeping the lid open.

Grilling Times

Estimated grilling times are just that—estimates. Every recipe gives an estimate of how long something will take to grill along with a recommended internal temperature or a description of the look of a food when that food is done. When cooking outdoors, the weather is always a factor; in cold or rainy weather, grilling times could be longer. In hot, sunny weather, they could be shorter.

In grilling, underdone is preferable to overcooked. If the food isn't quite done, it can always be put back on the grill or finished on the stovetop, in the oven, or in the microwave. If the food gets overcooked, there is no remedy.

An instant-read thermometer can be used to test the doneness of foods on the grill. The thermometer is inserted into the thickest part of the meat or poultry.

Doneness Chart for Grilling	
Burgers	130°F for rare, 145° to 150°F for medium, 160°F for well done
Beef steak	130°F for rare, 145° to 150°F for medium, 160°F for well done
Chicken breast	155° to 160°F for completely cooked
Chicken legs, thighs	160° to 165°F for completely cooked
Fish fillets or steaks	Begin to flake when tested with a fork in thickest part
Fruits	Done to your liking or slightly starting to caramelize
Lamb chops	130°F for rare, 145° to 150°F for medium, 160°F for well done
Pork loin or rib chops	145° to 150°F for medium, 160°F for well done
Pork tenderloin	130°F for rare, 145°to 150°F for medium, 160°F for well done
Shellfish	Opaque and somewhat firm to the touch
Veal chops	130° to 135°F for rare, 145° to 150°F for medium, 160°F for well done
Vegetables	Done to your liking

Specialty Grill Gadgets and Techniques

Once you have mastered the grilling basics, there are additional tools and techniques that you can add to your grilling repertoire. With the right equipment and grill gadgets, you can easily branch out into more sophisticated recipes, techniques and flavors. Here are some to consider.

Wooden Skewers: These should be soaked for about thirty minutes before using. Double-skewer foods for more control and to prevent the food from spinning on the skewer.

Flat Metal Skewers, Wire Kebab Skewers, and **Metal Kebab Baskets:** These work great, and don't require any soaking.

Metal Grill Woks: These are also perforated to let in smoky flavor. They are used to stir-grill pieces of fish, chicken, shellfish, other tender cubes of meat, and vegetables by tossing with wooden paddles.

Wood Planks: These planks (cedar is the strongest) impart an aromatic wood flavor to fish, shellfish, poultry, and vegetables.

Metal Plank Saver: This is a metal tray on which the plank is placed to keep the flames from charring it, if planking is done over direct heat.

Vertical Roaster: This is used to grill-roast a chicken, beer can style.

Grill-Top Pizza Stone: This makes the grill function like a pizza oven.

Fajita Pan: This corrals slices of beef or chicken, pepper, and onion so they all grill together without falling through the grates.

Stone Griddle or Piastra: These heat up on the grill so you can griddle-grill shellfish, chicken, fish, or steak to a fabulous finish.

Metal Grill Press: This flattens spatchcocked chicken (one that has the backbone removed and is pressed open) or Italian panini sandwiches to cook evenly on the grill.

Slider Maker and Grilling Basket: These allow you to make and grill small burgers for slider sandwiches.

Skewers

The old standby is the inexpensive wooden skewer (bamboo), which comes in packages at the grocery store. These skewers need to be soaked in cold water for at least thirty minutes before threading them with food and grilling. After grilling, the charred skewers are thrown away.

Reusable metal skewers come with prongs on both ends, or the new metal coil skewers can be easily cleaned after grilling with soapy water, then towel dried so they don't get water spots.

Kebab baskets are great time-savers, as the small pieces of cubed food are placed in the long basket rather than onto skewers. Brushing the inside of the baskets with oil before grilling helps keep foods from sticking.

Grill Woks

For stir-grilling, a metal grill wok with perforations plus wooden spoons, paddles, or long-handled spatulas is the basic equipment. The perforations in the grill wok allow for more of the wood and charcoal fire aromas to penetrate the foods. The long-handled utensils keep hands and arms safe while stir-grilling the food as it cooks.

Planks

Grilling food on a plank provides two flavors in one—the aromatic wood flavor of the plank and the flavor of the grill. Grilling planks come in a variety of sizes, from small planks for individual servings to larger planks that accommodate a whole salmon fillet. The only part of the food that gets the aromatic wood flavor from the plank is the surface that touches the wood, so flatter foods are better for planking: shrimp, scallops, boneless chicken breasts, fish fillets, portobello mushrooms, and baby Brie.

Planks need to be immersed in water for at least one hour before grilling. A water-soaked plank produces maximum smoke flavor and is more resistant to charring on the grill.

Planking starts with an indirect or dual-heat fire (high or medium-high on one side, low on the other). The foods are placed on the plank, the plank goes on the indirect side of the grill or the direct side if you're using a plank saver, and cooking is done with the grill closed.

Hardwoods for Planking

Alder gives a light, aromatic flavor and is great paired with fish.

Cedar is probably the most aromatic of the woods, lending a deep but gentle woodsy flavor to planked foods of all kinds.

Hickory lends a stronger, hearty wood flavor to beef, pork, or poultry.

Maple smolders to a sweeter, milder flavor that pairs well with poultry, vegetables, or fish.

Oak gives a medium, woodsy aroma without being bitter.

Roasters

Metal grill roasters allow foods from a whole chicken (without the beer can) to a chile pepper or stuffed apple to grill-roast over an indirect fire. The food is placed firmly on the roaster, then the roaster goes on the indirect or no-heat side of the grill, with the lid closed.

Rotisserie

Rotisserie cooking allows foods to grill-roast on a turning spit, usually done on a gas grill. Depending on the strength of the rotisserie equipment, the Thanksgiving turkey to whole chickens, fish, pork loin, or prime rib can go on the spit. Manufacturer's directions on your rotisserie attachment will tell you the maximum weight your spit can hold. Every gas grill has manufacturer's directions for the best way to set up the rotisserie on a grill. Basically, it's important to run through the setup before placing the food on the spit over a hot fire. With the grill off, the food should be measured over a disposable aluminum pan used to catch drips. This drip pan can be filled with two to three inches of liquid—water, beer, fruit juice, or wine—that can be used to flavor the food. The pan will prevent flare-ups, so it's important that the meat, chicken, or fish is not larger than the drip pan.

The meat, poultry, or fish, is trimmed accordingly, then seasoned. A rotisserie basket should be oiled first, then the food placed inside and closed firmly. One of the pronged attachments or spit forks is then slid onto the rotisserie rod with the attachment and clamp in position to tighten. Then the rod is slid through the center of the meat, fish, or fowl, with the second prong attachment so that the tines are touching the food. Both attachments should be pressed into the food on either side, so that the food is held firmly in place, with the clamps secured and tightened. Then the spit is balanced so it will turn evenly.

Next, the spit is placed on the rotisserie. The rotisserie switch is active, and it's smart to let the food rotate enough times until it's evident that it will turn easily. Then the drip pan is placed under the food and the grill lid closed to make sure it will close while the rotisserie is on. Check to make sure the lid will close while the rotisserie is on. Finally, the grill can be turned on so the temperature is close to 350°F.

Using Rubs, Marinades, Bastes, Mops, and Finishing Sauces

To get maximum deliciousness from grilled food, there are ways to add flavor and modify texture before, during, and after grilling.

Before grilling, foods can marinate in a boldly flavored liquid, usually a combination of a vegetable oil and an acid such as wine, beer, citrus juices, or vinegar plus garlic, herbs, spices, and condiments like Dijon mustard or Worcestershire sauce. Marinades are best for flatter foods like chicken breasts, flank steak, pork tenderloin, or fish fillets (only marinate fish for 30 minutes, as the acid in the marinade could "cook" the delicate fish). For increased tenderness and moist results, larger foods like a whole turkey, chicken, pork loin, or pork chops can be brined in a salty liquid often flavored with honey, maple syrup, sugar, and spices. For simple grilling, foods can be brushed with vegetable oil on both sides and sprinkled with a dry rub, which is any mixture of dry herbs and spices mixed with salt and pepper.

During grilling, a buttery baste can be brushed on to keep delicate foods moist. For barbecue sauce or other grilling sauces, it's best to sear the food first on both sides over direct heat, then move it to the indirect side of the grill and brush on the sauce. Most barbecue or grilling sauces have a high sugar content and will burn on the food over high heat. On the indirect side, the sauce will lacquer the food and develop a beautiful sheen.

After grilling, food can be served with any number of sauces, from pestos and aiolis (garlicky mayonnaise) to classic French béarnaise, potent Asian-style vinaigrettes, all-American barbecue sauce, South American chimichurri, or chocolate ganache for grilled fruit.

Appetizers

Planked
Big Easy Shrimp

SERVES 4

Grilling food on a hardwood plank is a great way to infuse it with the aromatic flavor of the wood. Simply prepare an indirect fire, arrange your food on the plank, place the plank on the indirect side, and cover the grill. Serve these succulent shrimp with grilled French bread for a taste of N'Awlins.

1   In a large bowl, combine the melted butter, seasoning, and barbecue sauce. Add the shrimp, toss to blend, and let marinate for 30 minutes in the refrigerator.

2   Prepare a moderate charcoal fire for indirect grilling (page xi), or preheat a gas grill to medium (375°F), leaving one of the burners unlit.

3   Remove the planks from the water and pat dry. Divide the shrimp between the planks, arranging them in one layer.

4   Place the planks over indirect heat. Cover the grill and cook for 10 to 15 minutes, or until the shrimp are pink and opaque.

5   Serve the shrimp from the planks or transfer to a serving platter.

Ingredients

2 cedar or oak grilling planks, soaked in water for at least 1 hour

4 tablespoons unsalted butter, melted

2 teaspoons blackened seasoning

2 tablespoons tomato-based barbecue sauce

1 pound large raw shrimp (27 to 30 count), peeled and deveined

Ingredients

2 to 2½ pounds fresh fava beans (to yield 2 cups shelled, unpeeled beans)

2 tablespoons extra virgin olive oil, plus more for garnish

1 large clove garlic, minced

9 fresh basil leaves

Kosher or sea salt and freshly ground black pepper

6 slices Italian country bread, about ½ inch thick and 3 inches long

Aged sheep's milk cheese (such as pecorino toscano, Manchego, or ricotta salata)

Grilled Bruschetta

with Fava Bean Puree and Pecorino

SERVES 6

At a spring dinner party, pass these irresistible toasts with the evening's first glass of white wine. The fava bean spread is moist and sweet and a fresh spring green, with aged sheep's milk cheese as its salty counterpoint.

1 Prepare a moderate charcoal fire or preheat a gas grill to medium.

2 Remove the fava beans from their pods. Bring a pot of water to a boil over high heat. Prepare a bowl of ice water. Add the fava beans to the boiling water and boil for 1½ minutes, or a little longer if the beans are large. Drain in a sieve or colander, then transfer to the ice water to stop the cooking. When the beans are cool, drain them again. To peel them, pierce the skin with your fingernail; the inner bean should slip out easily.

3 Heat 1 tablespoon of the olive oil in a small skillet over moderate heat. Add the garlic and sauté until fragrant, about 1 minute. Remove from the heat.

4 Put the peeled fava beans, the sautéed garlic, and all the oil in the skillet, three of the basil leaves, and the remaining 1 tablespoon olive oil in a small food processor. Pulse until nearly but not completely smooth; leave the spread slightly coarse. Transfer to a bowl and stir in salt and pepper to taste.

5   Grill the bread on both sides directly over
    the coals or gas flame until golden brown.
    Top each toast with some of the fava spread,
    dividing it evenly. Drizzle with some olive oil.
    Shave or grate some cheese over each toast.
    Garnish with a basil leaf. Serve immediately.

Grilled Mozzarella and Anchovies

in Chard Leaves

SERVES 4

The big, floppy leaves of Swiss chard make flexible wrappers for grilled foods—in this case, a slice of mozzarella, a pinch of oregano, and an anchovy fillet. Warmed over the fire, the chard crisps and the cheese melts. Set the seared package on a thick piece of toast and serve it as a knife-and-fork first course.

1   Prepare a moderate charcoal fire for indirect grilling (page xi) or preheat a gas grill to medium (375°F), leaving one burner unlit.

2   Separate the chard leaves from the ribs by cutting along the ribs with a sharp knife. Try to damage the leaves as little as possible.

3   Put the leaves in a large heatproof bowl and cover with boiling water. Let stand for 2 minutes. Drain in a sieve or colander and immediately run under cold running water until cool. Drain again and gently squeeze to remove excess moisture. Unfurl the chard leaves on a kitchen towel, shiny side down, and pat dry.

Ingredients

4 large Swiss chard leaves

6 ounces fresh whole-milk mozzarella cheese, in 4 equal slices

4 anchovy fillets

1 teaspoon dried oregano

Hot red pepper flakes

Pinch of kosher or sea salt

Extra virgin olive oil

4 slices Italian country bread, about ½ inch thick and 4 inches long

7

4   Put a slice of mozzarella in the center of each leaf. Top each slice with an anchovy fillet, ¼ teaspoon dried oregano (crumble it between your fingers as you add it), and a pinch each of hot pepper flakes and salt. Fold the bottom of each leaf over the cheese, fold in the sides, and then roll to form a neat package. Brush each package lightly all over with olive oil and sprinkle all over with salt.

5   Put the Swiss chard packets on the grill over indirect heat. Cook uncovered, turning once, until the packages feel squishy, indicating that the cheese inside has warmed enough to melt, 5 to 8 minutes total. While the chard cooks, brush the bread slices on both sides with olive oil. Place the bread on the grill directly over the coals or gas flame and toast on both sides.

6   Put a piece of toast on each plate. Top each toast with a Swiss chard bundle. Serve immediately.

Grilled Tomatillo Salsa

Ingredients

½ pound tomatillos (about 5 medium)

½ small white onion, peeled

1 or 2 cloves garlic, unpeeled

1 jalapeño chile

6 cilantro sprigs

Kosher or sea salt

MAKES ABOUT 1⅓ CUPS

Grilling all the vegetables for this salsa verde—"green salsa"—adds an alluring smoky note. Once you have grilled the components, you can make the salsa in a couple of minutes. Serve with Grilled Quesadillas (page 13), tacos, or chips, or as a garnish for corn soup. At the market, choose tomatillos that feel firm and have an intact husk.

1 Prepare a moderate charcoal fire or preheat a gas grill to medium (375°F). Remove the husks from the tomatillos and wash them to remove any stickiness. Dry well.

2 Grill the tomatillos, onion half, garlic, and chile directly over the coals or gas flame, turning as needed, until charred on all sides. They don't need to be thoroughly blackened, but they should have plenty of toasty char.

3 Put the tomatillos and onion in a blender. Peel the garlic and add to the blender along with the chile and cilantro. Blend until smooth. Transfer to a small bowl and stir in salt to taste. Thin to a pleasing consistency with a few tablespoons of water.

Ingredients

4 large eggs, at room temperature

3 tablespoons extra virgin olive oil

4 hearts of romaine, each 5 to 6 ounces, halved lengthwise with the core attached

Kosher or sea salt and freshly ground black pepper

Chunk of Parmigiano Reggiano cheese, for grating

4 lemon wedges

. . . .

Grilled Romaine

with a Six-Minute Farm Egg

SERVES 4

Why six minutes? Because that timing produces a picture-perfect boiled egg, with a firm white and a creamy, brilliant yellow yolk. If you have never grilled romaine hearts, a delightful surprise awaits. Thanks to their natural sugar, they color up beautifully on the grill. Cook them until they hover on the brink between tender and crisp. Shower with Parmigiano Reggiano and accompany with lemon wedges and your impeccable eggs. Serve as a first course or side dish for a grilled T-bone steak.

1   Prepare a moderate charcoal fire or preheat a gas grill to medium (375°F).

2   Put the eggs in a saucepan with water to cover by 1 inch. Bring to a boil over high heat, then immediately cover and set aside for 6 minutes exactly. Drain and quickly run under cold running water until cool, then peel and set aside.

3   Put the olive oil on a tray or platter. Turn the romaine hearts in the oil to coat them all over. Season with salt.

4   Place the romaine hearts directly over the coals or gas flame. Cook, turning as needed, until they are lightly browned on both sides, crisp in spots, and tender yet still a touch crunchy, 5 to 7 minutes.

5   Transfer the romaine hearts to a serving
    platter or individual plates. Grind some
    pepper over the romaine, then grate
    Parmigiano Reggiano over them, using as
    much as you like. Cut the eggs in half and
    place them alongside the romaine. Sprinkle
    a little salt on the eggs. Accompany with the
    lemon wedges. Serve immediately.

Grilled Quesadillas
with Mozzarella and Squash Blossoms

SERVES 4

Squash blossoms vary greatly in size depending on whether they come from zucchini or from winter squash. You can use small or large ones here. Some farmers sell baby zucchini with blossoms still attached. For this recipe, twist off the blossoms and reserve the zucchini for another dish.

1   Prepare a moderate charcoal fire or preheat a gas grill to medium (375°F). Tear the squash blossoms in half lengthwise and inspect for ants. Dunk the blossoms in a large bowl of cold water, swish well, then lift them out into a sieve or colander to drain. Pat dry. If the blossom halves are large, tear each one lengthwise into two or three pieces.

2   Heat the canola oil in a large skillet over moderately low heat. Add the onion, garlic, and oregano, crumbling the herb between your fingers as you add it. Sauté until the onion is soft, about 10 minutes. Add the squash blossoms, season with salt, and cook, stirring to coat them with the seasonings, just until the blossoms begin to soften, about 1 minute. Do not let them wilt.

3   Halve and pit the avocado. With a large spoon, scoop both halves out of the peel in one piece and put, cut side down, on a cutting board. Slice thinly lengthwise.

Ingredients

16 large or 24 small squash blossoms

2 tablespoons canola oil, plus more for brushing

1 small white onion, minced

2 cloves garlic, minced

1 teaspoon dried Mexican oregano

Kosher or sea salt

1 small avocado, ripe but firm

4 flour tortillas, 9 inches in diameter

½ pound low-moisture whole-milk mozzarella cheese, grated on the large holes of a box grater

Grilled Tomatillo Salsa (page 9)

Fresh cilantro leaves, for garnish

4   Brush one side of a flour tortilla with canola oil, then place it, oiled side down, on a rimless baking sheet. Top one-half of the tortilla with one-quarter of the cheese, then with one-quarter of the squash blossom mixture. Fold like a turnover. Repeat with the remaining tortillas. Slide the folded tortillas onto the grill directly over the coals or gas flame. Cook until browned on the bottom, about 1 minute, then turn and grill until the quesadilla browns on the second side and the cheese melts, about 1 minute longer.

5   Top each quesadilla with a drizzle of salsa, a few slices of avocado, and a sprinkling of cilantro leaves. Serve immediately.

Salads and Sandwiches

Fresh Farm Slaw

SERVES 6

This crunchy cabbage-based slaw incorporates farm-fresh raw vegetables all chopped and dressed with a vinaigrette lightly sweetened with honey. It is the perfect accompaniment for a summer lunch. Adapt it as you like, adding raw sweet peppers, carrots, kohlrabi, daikon, cucumbers, or turnips.

1   Chop the napa cabbage, green cabbage, radishes, and broccoli florets into small pieces roughly ¼ to ⅓ inch. The vegetables do not need to be precisely diced but should be about the same size. With a paring knife or vegetable peeler, pare the tough outer layer of the broccoli stalks to reveal the pale core. Chop the cores the same size as the other vegetables.

2   Put all the chopped vegetables in a large bowl and add the green onions and green beans. Toss to mix.

3   To make the dressing, in a bowl, whisk together the olive oil, vinegar, honey, ginger, and salt and pepper to taste. Taste and adjust the balance of sweet and tart. Add the dressing to the slaw, using only as much as you need to coat the vegetables nicely; you may not need it all. Toss well, taste, and adjust the seasoning. Let rest at room temperature for about an hour before serving, or cover and refrigerate if serving later. The slaw will remain crunchy for at least 8 hours.

Ingredients

½ pound napa cabbage, cored

½ pound green cabbage, cored

1 bunch red radishes (about 12 medium to large), trimmed

½ pound broccoli, florets separated from stalks

½ bunch green onions, pale and green parts, sliced ¼ inch thick

½ pound green beans, ends trimmed and sliced ¼ inch thick

Dressing

⅓ cup extra virgin olive oil

2½ tablespoons cider vinegar, or more to taste

1 tablespoon honey

¼ teaspoon ground ginger

Kosher or sea salt and freshly ground black pepper

Dressing

3 tablespoons extra virgin olive oil

1 tablespoon fresh lemon juice, or more if needed

1 large shallot, minced

Kosher or sea salt and freshly ground black pepper

9 figs, halved lengthwise

1 tablespoon unsalted butter, melted

½ pound mixed baby salad greens

¾ cup walnut halves, toasted (see note) and coarsely chopped

3 to 4 ounces blue cheese, firm enought to crumble

• • • • • • • • • • • • • • • • • • •

NOTE: For toasting walnuts and pecans, preheat the oven to 350°F. Spread the walnuts on a baking sheet and toast until fragrant and lightly colored, about 10 minutes. Let cool.

Baby Greens
with Grilled Figs, Blue Cheese, and Walnuts

SERVES 6

Warming figs on the grill seems to heighten their sweetness, slightly caramelizing their natural sugar. Serve them as a companion to blue cheese at the end of a meal or, as here, in a salad with crumbled blue cheese and toasted walnuts.

1 Prepare a moderate charcoal fire or preheat a gas grill to medium (375°F).

2 To make the dressing, in a small bowl, whisk together the olive oil, lemon juice, and shallot. Season to taste with salt and pepper.

3 Using wooden skewers, skewer the fig halves lengthwise, putting as many on a skewer as will fit. Brush lightly with the melted butter. Grill directly over the coals or gas flame, turning once, just until hot throughout.

4 Put the baby greens and walnuts in a large bowl. Add the blue cheese, crumbling it as you add it. Add just enough dressing to coat the greens lightly; you may not need it all. Toss to coat the greens evenly. Taste and adjust the seasoning. Add another squeeze of lemon, if needed.

5 Divide the salad among individual salad plates or arrange on a platter. Nestle the warm figs among the greens. Serve immediately.

Grilled Tuna Niçoise
with Anchovy Vinaigrette

SERVES 8

Salade niçoise exists for those days when you are inundated with summer vegetables. Replace the usual canned tuna with grilled fresh ahi, open a bottle of chilled rosé, and toast the farmers whose hard work enables this feast.

1 To make the anchovy vinaigrette, in a small bowl, whisk together the olive oil, vinegar, anchovies, garlic, capers, tarragon, and fish sauce. Season to taste with salt.

2 Preheat the oven to 375°F. If the beet greens are attached, remove all but ½ inch of the stem. Reserve the greens and stems for another use. Put the beets in a large baking dish, and add water to a depth of ¼ inch. Cover and bake until a knife pierces them easily, 45 minutes or longer, depending on their size. When cool enough to handle, peel the beets and cut into wedges.

3 Put the potatoes in a large pot and add salted water to cover by 1 inch. Bring to a boil over high heat, then reduce the heat to maintain a simmer and cook until tender when pierced, 15 to 20 minutes. Drain. When cool enough to handle, peel the potatoes and slice thickly.

Anchovy Vinaigrette

1 cup extra virgin olive oil

⅓ cup red wine vinegar, plus more if needed

12 anchovy fillets, minced to a paste

2 large cloves garlic, finely minced

2 tablespoons capers, preferably salt packed, rinsed and finely minced

1½ tablespoons chopped fresh tarragon

1½ tablespoons fish sauce (see note, page 23)

Kosher or sea salt

8 small or 4 medium beets

1½ pounds waxy potatoes such as fingerlings, unpeeled

1 pound slender green beans such as haricots verts, ends trimmed

4 large eggs

1¾ to 2 pounds ahi tuna steaks, about ¾ inch thick

Extra virgin olive oil

1½ teaspoons fennel seed, crushed in a mortar or spice grinder

1 heart of butter lettuce, separated into leaves (reserve outer leaves for another use)

4 large tomatoes, cut into wedges

1 pound cucumbers, peeled and cut into small chunks

16 radishes, trimmed

¾ cup unpitted Niçoise olives

4 Bring a large pot of salted water to a boil over high heat. Add the green beans and boil until they have lost their crispness but are still firm, about 5 minutes. Drain in a sieve or colander and immediately run under cold running water until cool. Drain again and pat thoroughly dry.

5 Put the eggs in a small saucepan with water to cover by 1 inch. Bring to a boil over high heat, then immediately cover and remove from the heat. Let stand for 6 minutes exactly. Drain and quickly run under cold running water until cool, then peel.

6 Prepare a moderate charcoal fire or preheat a gas grill to medium (375°F). Coat the tuna with olive oil, then season with salt and the fennel. Grill directly over the coals or gas flame, turning once, until the tuna is just cooked through, 4 to 5 minutes per side. Let cool to room temperature.

7 At serving time, line a large platter—or two platters if necessary—with the lettuce. By hand, break the tuna up into smaller pieces. Put it in a bowl and toss with enough of the vinaigrette to moisten it generously. Taste and adjust with more salt or vinegar as needed. Put the tuna in the center of the platter(s). Separately dress the beets, potatoes, green beans, tomatoes, and cucumbers with enough of the vinaigrette to coat them; taste and adjust with more salt or vinegar as needed. (You can use the same bowl each time.) Arrange the vegetables around the tuna in separate mounds. Cut the eggs in quarters lengthwise. Sprinkle the eggs and radishes with a little salt and arrange them around the vegetables, tucking them where you can. Scatter the olives over all. Serve immediately, passing any extra vinaigrette.

NOTE: Fish sauce is a clear, amber liquid made from salted and fermented anchovies or other small fish. In Vietnamese and Thai cooking, it is almost as ubiquitous as salt. Used with restraint, it adds depth and a highly savory note to many Western dishes, such as salad dressings. The widely available Three Crabs brand is excellent.

Ingredients

Pesto

1½ cups firmly packed fresh basil
leaves

2 cloves garlic, sliced

¼ cup pine nuts, toasted (see
note)

½ cup extra virgin olive oil

6 tablespoons freshly grated
Parmigiano Reggiano
or pecorino cheese, or a mix

Kosher or sea salt

2 small eggplants, about ½ pound
each

Kosher or sea salt

2 tablespoons extra virgin olive oil

4 pieces thick focaccia, halved
horizontally, or 8 pieces thin
focaccia, each roughly 3 by 6
inches or equivalent

8 to 12 thin tomato slices

6 ounces fresh whole-milk
mozzarella cheese, thinly silced

NOTE: To toast pine nuts, preheat
the oven to 325°F. Spread the
pine nuts on a baking sheet and toast
until fragrant and lightly colored,
8 to 10 minutes. Let cool.

Grilled Eggplant and Mozzarella Panini

SERVES 4

Here eggplant, tomato, and mozzarella meet in a panino, or Italian
sandwich. The sliced eggplant is grilled first, then layered with the
other ingredients between two pieces of pesto-brushed focaccia. After
another brief trip to the grill to crisp the bread and melt the mozzarella,
the hot panini are ready to slice and savor.

1   To make the pesto, put the basil, garlic, and pine nuts in a food
    processor and pulse until well chopped. With the motor running,
    add the olive oil gradually through the feed tube, stopping once
    or twice to scrape down the sides of the work bowl. Puree until
    the pesto is almost but not completely smooth. Transfer to a
    bowl and stir in the cheese. Season to taste with salt.

2   Slice off the eggplants' green cap, then cut each eggplant
    lengthwise into slices 3/16 inch thick. Discard the first and last
    slices, which are mostly skin. Sprinkle the remaining slices
    generously on both sides with salt. Place them on a rack and
    let stand for 30 minutes. Moisture will bead on the surface.

3   Prepare a moderate charcoal fire or preheat a gas grill to
    medium (375°F). Pat the eggplant slices dry with paper towels,
    then brush on both sides with 1 tablespoon of the olive oil.
    Place the slices directly over the coals or gas flame and cook,
    turning once, until just tender, about 3 minutes on per side.
    Remove from the grill.

4   Spread 1 tablespoon pesto on one side of each focaccia piece—on the cut side if you have halved the focaccia, or on the bottom side if you have not. Layer the grilled eggplant slices, overlapping them slightly, on four of the pesto-topped slices. Top the eggplant with the tomato slices, then with mozzarella, dividing them both evenly. Place another piece of focaccia, pesto side down, on the sandwich.

5   Brush the sandwiches with the remaining 1 tablespoon olive oil on both sides. Place the sandwiches directly over the coals or gas flame and cook, turning once, until they are hot throughout, the focaccia is nicely toasted, and the mozzarella is molten, about 3 minutes per side, depending on the heat of the fire. Cut in half and serve immediately.

Ingredients

2 medium green zucchini, as straight as possible

2 medium yellow zucchini, as straight as possible

2 tablespoons extra virgin olive oil, or more if needed

Kosher or sea salt

4 red onion slices, about ½ inch thick

4 pita breads, halved

1 cup Red Pepper Hummus

8 to 12 thin tomato slices

½ cup fresh cilantro leaves

Red Pepper Hummus

1 cup dried chickpeas

½ yellow onion

2 bay leaves

Kosher or sea salt

2 small red bell peppers

¼ cup tahini

¼ cup extra virgin olive oil

¼ cup fresh lemon juice, plus more to taste

2 cloves garlic, sliced

1 teaspoon cumin seed, toasted (see note) and finely ground

¼ teaspoon Spanish paprika, preferably the smoked pimentón de la Vera

Pita Sandwich

with Grilled Zucchini and Red Pepper Hummus

SERVES 4; MAKES 2⅔ CUPS HUMMUS

A pita pocket makes a handy holder for grilled vegetables of many types. Instead of the grilled zucchini suggested here, try grilled peppers, leeks, radicchio, or eggplant. You can also replace the hummus with guacamole, if you like. The leftover hummus is also great with lightly grilled pita bread.

1   Put the chickpeas in a medium bowl, add water to cover generously, and soak overnight. Drain and rinse, then put in a medium pot with cold water to cover by 1 inch. Bring to a simmer over moderate heat, skimming any foam. Add the onion half and bay leaves, cover, and adjust the heat to maintain a gentle simmer. Cook until the chickpeas are tender, 1 to 1½ hours. Season with salt and let cool in the liquid.

2   Prepare a moderate charcoal fire or preheat a gas grill to medium (375°F). Grill the peppers directly over the coals or gas flame, turning occasionally, until blackened on all sides. When cool enough to handle, peel the peppers and remove the stem and seeds. Cut each into quarters.

3   Drain the chickpeas and discard the onion and bay leaves. Place in a food processor along with the roasted peppers,

tahini, olive oil, lemon juice, garlic, cumin, and paprika and process until smooth. Season with salt and process again. Taste and add more lemon if desired. Serve immediately or cover and refrigerate for up to 1 week, bringing to room temperature before serving.

4 Trim the ends of the zucchini. Slice each one lengthwise about ³⁄₁₆ inch thick. Brush the slices with olive oil on both sides, then season with salt. From opposing directions, insert two toothpicks horizontally into each red onion slice; the toothpicks will hold the onion layers together on the grill. Brush the onion slices with olive oil on both sides, then season with salt.

5 Grill the zucchini and onion slices directly over the coals or gas flame, turning once, until they are nicely marked by the grill and just tender, about 3 minutes per side for the zucchini, a little longer for the onions. Remove the toothpicks from the onions. Cut the zucchini slices in half crosswise.

6 Wrap the pita in aluminum foil and warm the package on the grill or in a moderate oven until the bread is hot.

7 To assemble the sandwiches, spread the interior of each pita half with the hummus, using about 2 tablespoons per half. Tuck some zucchini, red onion, tomato, and cilantro leaves into each pita half, dividing them evenly. Serve immediately.

NOTE: For toasting cumin seed, put the whole cumin seed in a small, dry skillet over moderate heat. Cook, swirling the pan frequently, until the cumin begins to darken and the toasty fragrance becomes apparent. Let cool.

Grilled Goat Cheese Sandwich

with Asian Pears and Prosciutto

Ingredients

4 teaspoons unsalted butter, softened, plus 2 tablespoons, melted

8 slices dense country bread such as pugliese, about ½ inch thick

¼ pound fresh goat cheese, cream cheese, or mild blue cheese, at room temperature

1 Asian pear, peeled, quartered, cored, and thinly sliced

Freshly ground black pepper

4 thin slices prosciutto

MAKES 4 SANDWICHES

Asian pears vary greatly in color, size, and shape, with skins ranging from pale yellow to caramel. Even when ripe, they don't become soft and creamy like regular pears. Instead, they are as crunchy as an apple, but juicier. Slice them into salads or tuck a few thin wedges into a grilled cheese sandwich. Here, they are paired in a toasted sandwich with prosciutto and fresh goat cheese.

1   Prepare a moderate charcoal grill or preheat a gas grill to medium (375°F).

2   Using the softened butter, butter four slices of bread on one side only. Top the remaining four bread slices with the cheese, spreading it evenly. Top the cheese on each slice with three or four pear slices. Add a few grinds of black pepper, then top with the prosciutto. Put the buttered bread, buttered side down, over the prosciutto. Brush the sandwiches with melted butter on both sides.

3   Place the sandwiches directly over the coals or gas flame and cook, turning once, until the bread turns golden brown and the cheese softens, about 1 minute per side. Cut in half and serve immediately.

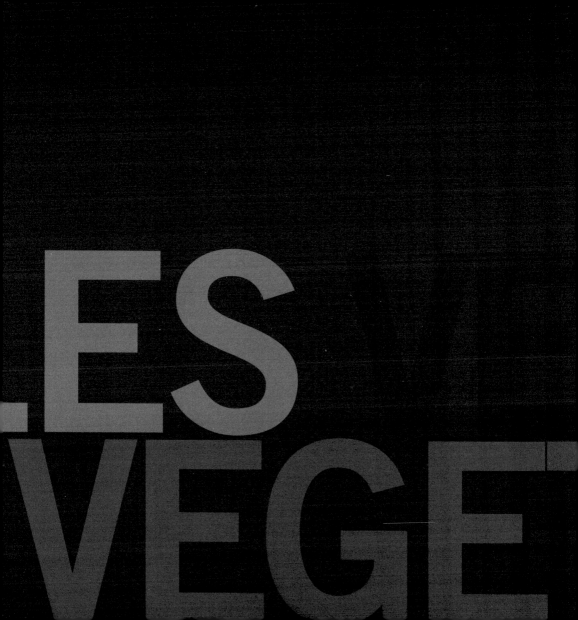

Vegetables

Grilled Corn

with Chipotle Butter and Cilantro

SERVES 4

Boiling corn leaves some of its natural sweetness behind in the water, while grilling corn intensifies its flavor. Grill the ears in the husk to steam the kernels, then peel back the husks and slather the ears with a spicy, smoky chipotle butter.

1   Prepare a moderately hot charcoal fire or preheat a gas grill to medium-high (375° to 400°F). Carefully peel back the corn husks without removing them, then pull out and discard the threadlike silk. Replace the corn husks and tie the tips closed with kitchen twine. Soak the ears in a sinkful of cold water for 20 minutes.

2   Put the butter in a small bowl. Add the chile and a large pinch of salt and stir to blend. Taste and add more salt or chile, if desired.

3   Place the corn directly over the coals or gas flame and cover the grill. Cook for about 15 minutes, giving the ears a quarter turn every 3 to 4 minutes as the husks brown.

4   Transfer the corn to a platter. Snip the ends of the husks to remove the twine tie. Remove and discard the husks. While the corn is hot, slather it with the chipotle butter, then sprinkle with the cilantro. Serve immediately.

Ingredients

4 ears corn

Chipotle Butter

4 tablespoons unsalted butter, softened

2 teaspoons finely minced canned chipotle chile in adobo sauce, or more to taste

Kosher or sea salt

2 tablespoons chopped fresh cilantro

Ingredients

Romesco

3 dried *ñora* chiles (see notes), or
   1 large dried New Mexico chile

2 plum (Roma type) tomatoes,
   about ½ pound total, quartered
   lengthwise

2 cloves garlic, peeled

5 tablespoons extra virgin olive oil

1 slice Italian country bread, about
   ½ inch thick and 4 inches long,
   crust removed

3 tablespoons whole natural
   almonds, toasted (see notes)

2 teaspoons sherry vinegar, or more
   to taste

1 teaspoon pimentón de la Vera
   (smoked Spanish paprika),
   medium or hot

¼ teaspoon cayenne pepper

Kosher or sea salt

12 small to medium leeks, white
   and pale green parts

6 tablespoons extra virgin olive oil

Kosher or sea salt

Grilled Leeks

with Romesco

SERVES 4 TO 6

In Spain's Catalonia region, people celebrate the harvest of *calçots*, the local sweet green onions, with an outdoor feast. The onions are blackened over a wood fire, wrapped in newspaper to steam until done, then unwrapped and served with romesco, the region's famous red pepper sauce. Leeks are not identical to *calçots*, but they are just as compatible with romesco, a sauce thickened with bread and almonds.

1   To prepare the romesco, stem and seed the chiles. Put the chiles in a small saucepan with just enough water to cover them. Bring to a simmer over high heat, then reduce the heat and simmer gently for 5 minutes. Cover the pan, remove from the heat, and let stand until cool.

2   Preheat the oven to 400°F. Put the tomatoes and garlic in a small baking dish just large enough to hold them. Drizzle with 1 tablespoon of the olive oil and turn them in the oil to coat them evenly. Bake until the tomatoes soften and begin to caramelize, about 30 minutes. Let cool.

3   Heat 1 tablespoon of the olive oil in a small skillet over moderate heat. Add the bread and fry until golden on both sides. Cool, then break into four or five pieces.

4 Put the softened chiles (reserving the soaking liquid), roasted tomatoes and garlic, bread, almonds, vinegar, *pimentón*, and cayenne in a food processor or blender. Process to a paste. With the motor running, add the remaining 3 tablespoons olive oil through the feed tube (or the hole in the blender lid), processing until the mixture is nearly smooth. Transfer to a bowl and stir in salt to taste. Thin, if desired, with some of the reserved chile-soaking liquid.

5 Prepare a moderate charcoal fire for indirect grilling (page xi) or preheat a gas grill to medium (375°F), leaving one burner unlit. Trim the root end of each leek, but keep the base intact to hold the leek together. Slice the leeks in half lengthwise and wash well between the layers. Dry thoroughly.

6 Put the 6 tablespoons of olive oil on a tray or platter. Turn the leeks in the oil to coat them all over. Season with salt. Place the leeks over indirect heat, cover, and cook, turning once, until the leeks are soft and both sides are nicely colored, about 15 minutes. If necessary, put them directly over the coals or gas flame for the last couple of minutes, uncovered, to char them slightly. Serve hot or warm with a dollop of romesco, or pass the sauce separately.

NOTES: Dried *ñora* chiles may be ordered from www.latienda.com.

For toasting almonds, preheat the oven to 350°F. Spread the almonds on a baking sheet and toast until fragrant and golden brown inside, about 8 minutes for sliced almonds, 12 to 15 minutes for whole almonds. (Break one open to check.) Let cool.

Ingredients

5 pounds ripe red tomatoes, coarsely chopped (no need to peel)

2 cups finely chopped yellow onion

2 cups finely chopped red bell pepper

¼ cup minced fresh Italian parsley

4 cloves garlic, finely chopped

2 tablespoons kosher or sea salt

2 bay leaves

1 whole clove

1 teaspoon yellow mustard seed

1 teaspoon whole allspice

1 teaspoon coriander seed

1 teaspoon black peppercorns

1 cinnamon stick

¼ cup honey

2 tablespoons cider vinegar

Garden Ketchup

MAKES 1½ PINTS

Making your own ketchup is a special touch for any grilled meal. This richly spiced tomato ketchup utilizes the freshest produce and seasonings of the season. It will keep for up to one year, so you can share the freshest flavors of summer year round.

1 Put the vegetables, parsley, garlic, and salt in a large pot. Bring to a simmer over moderate heat, stirring occasionally. Adjust the heat to maintain a brisk simmer and cook until the tomatoes are soft, about 30 minutes. Pass the mixture through a food mill fitted with the fine disk and return the puree to the pot.

2 Put the bay leaves, clove, mustard seed, allspice, coriander seed, peppercorns, and cinnamon stick on a square of cheesecloth, then tie with kitchen twine to make a spice bag. Add to the pot with the honey. Simmer over moderate heat, stirring occasionally, until the mixture has reduced by half, about 1 hour. Remove the spice bag and add the vinegar. Continue to simmer, stirring as needed to prevent sticking, until the mixture reaches the desired thickness, or about 3 cups.

3 Fill a canning kettle with enough water to cover three half-pint canning jars (or one pint jar and one half-pint jar) resting on the preserving rack. Bring to a boil. Wash the jars with hot, soapy water; rinse well, and keep upside down on a clean dish towel until you are ready to fill them. Put three new lids (never reuse lids) in a heatproof bowl and cover with boiling water.

4   Using a ladle and a funnel, transfer the ketchup to the jars, leaving ½ inch headspace. Wipe the rims clean with a damp paper towel. Top with lids and then a screw band. Close tightly.

5   Place the jars on the preserving rack and lower it into the canning kettle. If the water doesn't cover the jars, add boiling water from a tea kettle. Cover the canning kettle. After the water returns to a boil, boil for 15 minutes. With a jar lifter, transfer the jars to a rack to cool completely. Do not touch the jars again until you hear the pops that indicate that the lids have sealed. You can confirm that a lid has sealed by pressing the center with your finger. If it gives, it has not sealed and the contents should be refrigerated and used within a week. Store the sealed jars in a cool, dark place for at least 2 weeks before using. They will keep for up to 1 year before opening. Refrigerate after opening.

Sweet Potatoes

on the Grill

Ingredients

4 sweet potatoes, each about 10 ounces

Unsalted butter

Kosher or sea salt and freshly ground black pepper

Whole nutmeg, for grating

SERVES 4

Add these sweet potatoes to the menu when you're grilling pork chops or a pork tenderloin. They can cook alongside the meat and need no attention, other than an occasional turn to prevent the skin from blackening. They need to cook with the grill lid on so that the grill emulates an oven. You can use moist, orange-fleshed sweet potatoes (sometimes called yams), but the Japanese varieties with pale, dry flesh are even tastier because they are not candy-sweet. Cooked this way, the drier varieties taste almost like roasted chestnuts.

1 Prepare a moderate charcoal fire for indirect grilling (page xi) or preheat a gas grill to medium-high (375° to 400°F), leaving one burner unlit.

2 Prick each sweet potato in several places with a fork. Place them on the grill over indirect heat. Cover the grill (leaving the vents open on a charcoal grill) and cook, turning occasionally, until the sweet potatoes are tender when pierced, 40 to 45 minutes.

3 Slit each sweet potato and tuck a large nugget of butter inside. Season with salt, a couple of grinds of black pepper, and a scraping of nutmeg. Serve immediately.

Grilled Cauliflower Steaks

with Tahini Sauce

Ingredients

Tahini Sauce
¼ cup tahini, stirred well to blend
¼ cup water
2 to 3 tablespoons fresh
    lemon juice
1 large clove garlic, minced
1 tablespoon minced fresh cilantro
Kosher or sea salt

2 medium cauliflowers
Extra virgin olive oil
Kosher or sea salt and freshly
    ground black pepper
Chopped fresh cilantro, for garnish

SERVES 4

From each head of cauliflower, you can cut two thick "steaks," slicing from top to bottom near the center to yield a pair of slices each held together by the core. The resulting "steaks," seared on the grill, make a head-turning presentation with a creamy tahini sauce. Use any leftover sauce on grilled vegetables, fish, or roasted beets.

1   Prepare a moderate charcoal fire for indirect grilling (page xi) or preheat a gas grill to medium (375°F), leaving one burner unlit.

2   To make the tahini sauce, in a small bowl, whisk together the tahini, ¼ cup water, and 2 tablespoons lemon juice until smooth. Whisk in the garlic, cilantro, and salt to taste. Taste and adjust with more lemon juice, if desired.

3   Trim each cauliflower, removing any leaves and cutting the stem flush with the base. Set a cauliflower, cut side down, on a cutting board. With a chef's knife, cut two "steaks," each about ¾ inch thick, from the center of the cauliflower, so that the core holds each slice together. Repeat with the second cauliflower. Reserve the remaining cauliflower for another use.

4   Put the four cauliflower steaks on a tray
    and brush one side with the olive oil. Season
    with salt and pepper. Turn the steaks over,
    brush the second side, and season with salt
    and pepper.

5   Place the steaks over indirect heat, cover
    the grill, and cook, turning once, until tender
    when pierced, about 15 minutes total. For
    the final minute or so of cooking, uncover the
    grill and move the cauliflower directly over the
    coals or flame to char it slightly.

6   Transfer the steaks to a platter and drizzle
    with the tahini sauce; you may not need it all.
    Garnish with cilantro and serve hot or warm.

Grilled Tomatoes
with Pesto

SERVES 4

This recipe yields more pesto than you need for the tomatoes, but why make just a little? You will have enough pesto left over to sauce ¾ pound of pasta the next day, a head start on dinner for four. Serve the tomatoes with grilled fish or steak.

1   Prepare a moderate charcoal fire or preheat a gas grill to medium (375°F).

2   To make the pesto, put the basil, garlic, and pine nuts in a food processor and pulse until well chopped. With the motor running, add the olive oil gradually through the feed tube, stopping once or twice to scrape down the sides of the work bowl. Puree until the pesto is almost but not completely smooth. Transfer to a bowl and stir in the cheese. Season to taste with salt.

3   Core the tomatoes. Slice off the rounded top and bottom of each tomato, then cut the remainder into ¾-inch-thick slices. Brush with olive oil on both sides and sprinkle on both sides with salt.

4   Grill the tomatoes directly over the coals or gas flame, turning once, just until hot throughout, 2 to 3 minutes per side. Do not overcook or they will become mushy. Transfer the tomato slices to a serving platter and slather them with the pesto, using 1 heaping teaspoon per slice (reserve the remaining pesto for another use), and serve immediately.

Ingredients

Pesto

1½ cups firmly packed fresh basil leaves

2 cloves garlic, sliced

¼ cup pine nuts, toasted (see note)

½ cup extra virgin olive oil

6 tablespoons freshly grated Parmigiano Reggiano or pecorino cheese, or a mix

Kosher or sea salt

3 large, firm tomatoes, 10 to 12 ounces each

1 tablespoon extra virgin olive oil

Kosher or sea salt

NOTE: To toast pine nuts, preheat the oven to 325°F. Spread the pine nuts on a baking sheet and toast until fragrant and lightly colored, 8 to 10 minutes. Let cool.

Ingredients

1 pound asparagus

2 teaspoons extra virgin olive oil

Kosher or sea salt

1 tablespoon citrus oil, such as
   Meyer lemon or blood orange oil

Grilled Asparagus
with Citrus Oil

SERVES 4

Many specialty stores and well-stocked supermarkets now carry aromatic oils made by pressing olives together with lemons, blood oranges, limes, or other citrus. Just a drizzle of one of these highly perfumed oils can make grilled vegetables seem dressed up for company. Serve with fish, roast chicken, or a steak.

1   Prepare a moderate charcoal fire for indirect grilling (page xi) or preheat a gas grill to medium (375°F), leaving one burner unlit.

2   To trim the asparagus, hold each spear horizontally between both hands and bend it. It will snap naturally at the point at which the spear becomes tough. Discard the tough end.

3   Put the trimmed asparagus spears on a platter and toss with the olive oil, which should just coat them lightly. Sprinkle with salt and toss again.

4   Place the spears over indirect heat, taking care to place them perpendicular to the bars of the grill rack so they do not fall through. Cover the grill and cook, turning the spears once halfway through, until almost tender, 4 to 5 minutes total. For the final minute or so of cooking, move the spears directly over the coals or gas flame and cook uncovered to char them slightly.

5   Transfer the spears to a serving platter and drizzle with the citrus oil. Toss to coat them evenly. Taste for salt. Serve immediately.

Grilled Carrots
with Fresh Thyme

········· ··········
Ingredients

1 pound slender carrots (about 6), well scrubbed but not peeled

1 tablespoon extra virgin olive oil

2 teaspoons finely minced fresh thyme

Kosher or sea salt
··········· ·········

SERVES 4

Who knew that carrots responded so happily to grilling? The dry heat of the grill concentrates their flavor, so they taste almost like a sweet potato. Serve these supersweet carrots with a pork roast or add to a platter of grilled vegetables.

1   Prepare a moderate charcoal fire for indirect grilling (page xi) or preheat a gas grill to medium (375°F), leaving one burner unlit.

2   If the carrots are uniformly slender, leave them whole. If they are considerably thicker at the top than at the bottom, cut them crosswise into 3- to 4-inch lengths and halve the thick ends to make pieces of about the same size.

3   Put the carrots on a platter, drizzle with the olive oil, and then roll the carrots to coat them lightly and evenly. Season with thyme and salt.

4   Place the carrots over indirect heat, cover the grill, and cook, turning occasionally, until the carrots have softened, about 20 minutes. For the final minute or so of cooking, uncover and move the carrots directly over the coals or gas flame to char them slightly. Serve hot.

Bagna Cauda

½ cup extra virgin olive oil

8 large cloves garlic, minced

8 anchovy fillets, finely minced

3 tablespoons extra virgin olive oil

2 heads radicchio, about ½
 pound each, quartered through
 the core and leaving the core
 attached

Kosher or sea salt

Minced fresh Italian parsley,
 for garnish

4 lemon wedges

Grilled Radicchio
with Bagna Cauda

SERVES 4

What Italians know as *bagna cauda*—literally, "hot bath"—is the world's most aromatic dip: hot olive oil with anchovies and garlic melted in it. Although Italians typically dunk raw vegetables, such as fennel or celery, into *bagna cauda*, in this recipe it is used as a sauce. Because you need a generous portion of oil to cover the garlic in the pan, it is easier to make a large quantity of *bagna cauda* than it is to make a small amount. Reserve the remainder for tossing with pasta or spooning over boiled broccoli rabe, cauliflower, or spinach or a grilled steak. It will keep refrigerated for 1 week.

1 Prepare a moderate charcoal fire for indirect grilling (page xi) or preheat a gas grill to medium (375°F), leaving one burner unlit.

2 To make the *bagna cauda*, put the ½ cup of olive oil and garlic in a small saucepan and place over low heat. Cook until the garlic is very soft and fragrant, about 30 minutes. Remove from the heat, add the anchovies, and stir until the anchovies dissolve. Return the saucepan to low heat and keep warm.

3 Put the 3 tablespoons of olive oil on a tray or platter. Turn the radicchio wedges in the oil to coat them all over. Season with salt.

4 Place the radicchio over indirect heat, cover the grill, and cook, turning occasionally, until softened and crisp in parts, about 10 minutes.

5 Transfer the radicchio to a platter and drizzle with the warm *bagna cauda*, using about half of it and reserving the remainder for another use. Garnish with the parsley and accompany with the lemon wedges. Serve immediately.

Ingredients

1 pound pattypan squashes

1 tablespoon olive oil

2 teaspoons dried Mexican oregano

Kosher or sea salt

¼ pound Mexican-style chorizo

2 tablespoons *crema*, crème fraîche, or sour cream

2 tablespoons coarsely chopped fresh cilantro

⅓ cup freshly grated Cotija or pecorino romano cheese

Grilled Pattypan Squash
with Chorizo and Cotija Cheese

SERVES 4

The scallop-edged summer squashes known as pattypan or scallopini are ideal for this preparation because, halved horizontally, their broad surface begs for a topping. Grill the squashes, then garnish with *crema* (Mexican-style cultured cream), warm crumbled chorizo, and grated Cotija cheese to make a summer side dish for grilled chicken or a main dish accompanied by rice and beans.

1   Prepare a moderate charcoal fire for indirect grilling (page xi) or preheat a gas grill to medium-high (375° to 400°F), leaving one burner unlit.

2   Trim the ends from the squashes so they will sit upright, then cut in half horizontally. Brush on both sides with the olive oil. Season both sides with the oregano, crumbling it between your fingers as you add it, and with salt.

3   Remove the chorizo from its casing and crumble into a small, nonstick skillet on the stove. Cook over moderately low heat, stirring, until the chorizo is fully cooked, 5 to 7 minutes. Keep warm.

4   Place the squash halves on the grill over indirect heat, cover, and cook, turning to brown both sides, until tender, about 20 minutes. Uncover the grill and move the squashes directly over the coals or gas flame for the final few minutes to color them nicely, if necessary.

5 Transfer to a serving platter. Whisk the *crema* until it is pourable, adding a little water if necessary. Drizzle over the squash halves. Top with the hot chorizo, then with the cilantro and cheese. Serve immediately.

Ingredients

1 pound fingerling potatoes,
  unpeeled

1 tablespoon extra virgin olive oil

Kosher or sea salt

¼ cup *crema* or sour cream

Ancho chile powder or other
  chile powder

1 tablespoon minced fresh cilantro

Grilled Fingerling Potatoes

with Crema and Chile Powder

SERVES 4

Waxy fingerling potatoes like Russian Banana and Rose Finn Apple respond beautifully to grilling. Boil them first, then halve and sear them until they are golden brown and crusty all over. Drizzle them with *crema*, the thick cultured cream sold in Mexican markets, and sprinkle with chile powder to give them a Mexican accent. Serve with a grilled skirt steak, chicken, or ribs.

1   Prepare a moderate charcoal fire or preheat a gas grill to medium (375°F).

2   Put the potatoes in a medium pot and add water to cover by 1 inch and bring to a boil over high heat. Reduce the heat to maintain a simmer and cook just until you can pierce the potatoes easily, about 15 minutes. Drain and let cool. Cut in half lengthwise.

3   Brush the potatoes all over with the olive oil and season with salt. Place, cut side down, directly over the coals or gas flame and grill until richly browned, about 5 minutes. Turn the potatoes and grill on the skin side until nicely crisped, about 5 minutes longer.

4   Place the potatoes, cut side up, on a serving platter. In a small bowl, whisk the *crema* with just enough water to make it pourable. Drizzle the *crema* over the potatoes, then sprinkle with chile powder to taste and garnish with the cilantro. Serve immediately.

Ingredients

Vinaigrette

6 tablespoons extra virgin olive oil

¼ cup red wine vinegar

1 clove garlic, grated or pressed

½ teaspoon coarse salt

Freshly ground black pepper

3 medium (about 5 ounces each) zucchini

Coarse salt

1 tablespoon minced fresh oregano

2 tablespoons finely slivered olive oil–packed sun-dried tomatoes, drained and patted dry, for garnish

Marinated Grilled Zucchini
with Oregano and Dried-Tomato Vinaigrette

SERVES 4

Zucchini is mild flavored, so it is the perfect canvas for the bold tastes of fresh oregano and dried tomatoes. Use your best extra virgin olive oil and aged red wine vinegar for the dressing.

1   In a small bowl, combine the olive oil, vinegar, garlic, salt, and a grinding of black pepper, and whisk until blended.

2   Trim the stem and blossom ends from the zucchini. With a mandoline or chef's knife, cut each zucchini lengthwise into five slices each about ¼ inch thick, and then spread the slices in a single layer on a platter.

3   Prepare a medium charcoal fire or preheat a gas grill to medium (350° to 400°F).

4   Brush the zucchini slices on both sides with a film of the vinaigrette. Working in batches, place the zucchini on the grill for 4 minutes, or until grill marks appear. Turn with tongs and grill the other side for 4 minutes, or until tender. As each batch is cooked, return the slices to the platter.

5 Sprinkle the zucchini slices lightly with salt. Whisk the oregano into the remaining vinaigrette and drizzle on top of the zucchini. Sprinkle with the tomato slivers. Serve warm or at room temperature.

Main Dishes

Grilled Country Pork Chops

with Bourbon-Basted Grilled Peaches

Ingredients

Brine

1½ quarts water

6 tablespoons kosher or sea salt

1 teaspoon coarsely cracked black pepper

Handful of thyme sprigs

2 cloves garlic, peeled and smashed with the side of a chef's knife

4 bone-in pork loin chops, about ¾ inch thick

2 tablespoons unsalted butter

2 tablespoons bourbon

2 teaspoons honey

2 large freestone peaches (such as O'Henry or Elberta), halved and pitted

SERVES 4

Grilling gives peaches and other stone fruits a flavor boost, bringing their natural sugar to the fore. Use freestone peaches so that you can easily twist the halves off the pit. Baste them with butter, honey, and bourbon as they grill to give them a sheen, then serve with a juicy pork chop, brined for a full day to season it all the way through.

1   To make the brine, in a medium saucepan, combine all the ingredients. Bring to a boil over high heat, stirring to dissolve the salt. Set aside until completely cool.

2   Put the pork chops in a container that holds them snugly in a single layer. Add the brine, which should cover them. Cover with plastic wrap. Alternatively, you can put the pork and its brine in a 1-gallon heavy-duty resealable food storage bag. Refrigerate for 24 hours.

3   About 1 hour before cooking, remove the pork chops from the brine and set them on a wire cooling rack at room temperature to dry.

4   Prepare a moderate charcoal fire for indirect grilling (page xi) or preheat a gas grill to medium (375°F), leaving one burner unlit.

5 Combine the butter, bourbon, and honey in a small saucepan. Set over moderately low heat, stirring until the butter melts and the honey dissolves. Keep warm.

6 Pat the pork chops with paper towels to remove any remaining surface moisture. Set the chops directly over the coals or gas flame and brown on both sides, turning once, for about 3 minutes per side. Transfer to indirect heat, cover the grill, and cook until the chops offer some resistance to the touch but are still springy, not firm, about 4 minutes longer. If you are unsure of doneness, measure the internal temperature with an instant-read thermometer, inserting it horizontally into a chop; it should register about 150°F for medium.

7 Once you have moved the pork chops to indirect heat, you can grill the peaches. Brush them all over with the butter-honey mixture and place, cut side down, directly over the coals or gas flame. Cook until they are nicely charred, then turn, baste again, and cook just until they are tender and juicy. The pork chops and peaches should be done at roughly the same time, but if not, move whichever is done first to a cooler area of the grill to wait. Serve each pork chop with a grilled peach half alongside.

Planked Salmon
with Mustard-Dill Glaze

SERVES 6

Planked fish is one of the easiest, most foolproof ways to grill seafood. It won't fall through the grill grate, and no turning is necessary. Planking fish adds two flavors—the aromatic wood flavor of the plank (usually cedar or alder for fish) as well as the flavor of the grill. A glaze brushed on the fish ensures a moist finished dish—and it's a built-in sauce!

1 To make the glaze, combine the mustard, mayonnaise, and dill weed in a small bowl until smooth.

2 Prepare a moderate charcoal fire for indirect grilling (page xi) or preheat a gas grill to medium (375°F), leaving one of the burners unlit.

3 Remove the plank from the water and pat dry. Trim the salmon fillet, if necessary, to fit the plank. Place the salmon on the prepared plank, season to taste, and spread the flesh side (the lighter, skinless side) with the glaze. Arrange fresh dill fronds on top of the glaze.

4 Place the plank over indirect heat. Cover the grill and cook until the fish begins to flake when tested with the tip of a small knife in the thickest part, 25 to 30 minutes.

5 Serve the salmon hot, right from the plank.

Ingredients

Mustard-Dill Glaze
½ cup Dijon mustard
½ cup mayonnaise
1 teaspoon dried dill weed
Fresh dill fronds for garnish

1 (1½-to 2-pound) salmon fillet, about ¾ inch thick, skin removed
Salt and pepper
1 cedar or alder grilling plank, soaked in water for at least 1 hour

Grilled Pizza

with Mozzarella, Arugula, and Chile Oil

MAKES 1 PIZZA; SERVES 2 TO 4

Wispy leaves of young arugula are used like an herb in this recipe, sprinkled on the sizzling pizza just as it comes off the grill. Note the long, slow rise on the dough—a total of six hours—which produces a particularly light, chewy, and flavorful crust.

1   To make the dough, put the warm water in a bowl and sprinkle the surface with the yeast. Let stand for 2 minutes to soften, then whisk with a fork to blend. Let stand until bubbly, about 10 minutes. Whisk in the olive oil and salt, then begin adding 1½ cups of the flour gradually, beating with a wooden spoon until fully incorporated. The dough will be very moist and sticky.

2   Turn the dough out on a lightly floured work surface and knead with floured hands until smooth and elastic, about 5 minutes, incorporating as much of the remaining ¼ cup of flour as needed to keep the dough from clinging to your hands or the work surface. The dough will remain moist and a little tacky but should not be sticky. Shape into a ball. Oil a bowl, transfer the dough to it, and turn the dough to coat it with oil. Cover the bowl with plastic wrap and let the dough rise at room temperature for 2 hours.

······················

Ingredients

Dough

¾ cup warm (105° to 115°F) water

1½ teaspoons active dry yeast

1 tablespoon olive oil, plus more for the bowl

1 teaspoon kosher or sea salt

About 1¾ cups unbleached all-purpose flour

Chile Oil

2 tablespoons extra virgin olive oil

1 large clove garlic, finely minced

¼ teaspoon hot red pepper flakes

Pinch of kosher or sea salt

½ teaspoon dried oregano

Cornmeal, for dusting the pizza peel

½ pound low-moisture whole-milk mozzarella cheese, grated on the large holes of a box grater

Large handful of baby arugula

······················

3 Punch the dough down. Reshape into a ball, re-cover the bowl, and let the dough rise again for 4 hours.

4 If using a charcoal grill, prepare a moderate fire. When the coals are ready, arrange them in an even layer on one-half of the grill bed.

5 If using a gas grill, preheat all burners to high. About 15 minutes before grilling, put a baking stone on the grill rack. The internal temperature of the grill should be 575° to 600°F.

6 Punch the dough down, turn it out onto a lightly floured work surface, and shape into a ball. Dust the surface of the dough with flour, cover with a dish towel, and let rest for 30 minutes.

7 To make the chile oil, in a small bowl, whisk together the olive oil, garlic, hot pepper flakes, and salt. Add the oregano, crumbling it between your fingers as you do, and whisk again. Let stand for 30 minutes to blend the flavors.

8 If you are using a round kettle grill with charcoal, you will need to shape the dough into a rectangle so that you can cook the crust first directly over the bed of coals, then flip it and finish cooking it over indirect heat. If you are using a gas grill with a baking stone, you can shape the dough into a circle because you will not need to flip it.

9 Dust a pizza peel or rimless baking sheet generously with cornmeal. To prepare the dough for topping, you can stretch it with a rolling pin or your hands. Lightly flour a work surface. To use a pin, roll out the dough on the floured surface into a 13- to 14-inch circle or into a roughly 16 by 10-inch rectangle, depending on your grill. Transfer to the prepared peel. To work by hand, flatten the dough into a round, then drape the round over the back of your two flour-dusted hands. Form your hands into fists and rotate the dough on your fists. The dough is supple enough that it will stretch with little effort on your part. Stretch into a 13- to 14-inch circle or into a roughly 16 by 10-inch rectangle, depending on your grill. Transfer to the prepared pizza peel.

10 If you are grilling the pizza over charcoal, slide the dough off onto the grill rack, directly over the coals. Cook uncovered until the dough begins to puff and blister and the bottom becomes nicely browned or even lightly charred in spots, 1 to 2 minutes. With tongs or your hands, flip the dough over onto the half of the grill with no coals. Working quickly, top with the cheese, spreading it evenly but leaving a ¾-inch rim uncovered. Brush the rim with the chile oil, then drizzle more of the oil, including the garlic and herbs, over the pizza, reserving a little oil for brushing the pizza rim after grilling.

Cover the grill and cook until the pizza rim is well browned and the cheese is melted and bubbling, about 5 minutes. Transfer the pizza to a cutting board, scatter the arugula over the cheese, and brush the rim with the remaining chile oil. Cut into wedges and serve immediately.

If you are grilling the pizza in a gas grill on a preheated baking stone, top the round of dough with the cheese, spreading it evenly but leaving a ¾-inch rim uncovered. Work quickly so the dough does not stick to the peel. Brush the rim with the chile oil, then drizzle more of the oil, including the garlic and herbs, over the pizza, reserving a little oil for brushing the pizza rim after grilling. Raising the lid of the grill as little as possible to avoid loss of heat, slide the pizza onto the baking stone and quickly close the grill. Cook until the crust smells well browned, even a little charred, 5 to 6 minutes; resist the urge to open the grill beforehand or you will release too much heat. Transfer the pizza to a cutting board, scatter the arugula over the cheese, and brush the rim with the remaining chile oil. Cut into wedges and serve immediately.

Ingredients

Glaze

2 tablespoons tamari

1 teaspoon toasted sesame oil

1 teaspoon peeled, grated fresh ginger

¼ teaspoon grated fresh garlic

4 (6-ounce) halibut steaks, about ½ inch thick

Chopped Mango, Ginger, and Sweet Onion Salad

1 tablespoon unseasoned rice vinegar

1 teaspoon tamari

½ teaspoon toasted sesame oil

½ teaspoon peeled, grated fresh ginger

¼ teaspoon grated fresh garlic

1 cup (¼-inch-dice) ripe mango

1 cup (¼-inch-dice) sweet onion

¼ cup (¼-inch-dice) red bell pepper

2 tablespoons finely chopped fresh cilantro

½ teaspoon minced jalapeño chile, or to taste (optional)

Tamari-Glazed Halibut

with Chopped Mango, Ginger, and Sweet Onion Salad

SERVES 4

This versatile recipe can be used to prepare almost any variety of fish. Steaks work best because of their uniform thickness, so try tuna, mahi mahi, salmon, or escolar. The salad is just as versatile. Try papaya, peach, or nectarine in place of the mango; red onion or green onion for the sweet onion; or basil for the cilantro. Tamari is a bit thicker and has a milder taste than soy sauce, so it makes a better glaze. But in a pinch, soy sauce may be substituted. Accompany the halibut with basmati, sushi, or other fragrant rice.

1 In a small bowl, whisk the tamari, sesame oil, ginger, and garlic until blended. Place the halibut steaks in a single layer on a large plate and brush with half of the glaze. Turn the steaks and brush with the remaining glaze. Refrigerate for 20 minutes. Meanwhile, prepare the salad.

2 In a medium bowl, combine the rice vinegar, tamari, sesame oil, ginger, and garlic, and stir until blended. Add the mango, onion, red bell pepper, cilantro, and chile. Using a rubber spatula, fold gently until well blended. Set aside until serving.

3 Prepare a medium-high charcoal fire or preheat a gas grill to medium-high (400°F). Cook the halibut for 3 minutes, adjusting the heat back to medium after 1 minute. Use a wide, flexible

spatula to turn the fish over. Cook for 3 minutes more, or until the fish is almost firm to the touch, or until the center is opaque, rather than translucent, when tested with the tip of a small knife.

4 Transfer the steaks to a serving platter, top each steak with an equal amount of the salad, and serve.

Ingredients

2 large globe eggplants, 1¼ to 1½ pounds each

Kosher or sea salt

2 tablespoons extra virgin olive oil

Tomato Sauce

¼ cup extra virgin olive oil

½ yellow onion, minced

2 large cloves garlic, minced

1½ pounds plum (Roma type) tomatoes, chopped (no need to peel)

8 to 12 fresh basil leaves

1 teaspoon dried oregano

Pinch of hot red pepper flakes

Kosher or sea salt

Ricotta Filling

2 cups whole-milk ricotta cheese (or one 15-ounce container)

½ cup freshly grated pecorino or Parmigiano Reggiano cheese

⅓ cup minced prosciutto

2 tablespoons minced fresh Italian parsley

1 large clove garlic, minced

Freshly ground black pepper

1 large egg, lightly beaten

½ cup freshly grated pecorino or Parmigiano Reggiano cheese, for topping

Grilled Eggplant Cannelloni

with Ricotta and Prosciutto

SERVES 4 AS A MAIN COURSE, OR 6 AS A FIRST COURSE

Lengthwise slices from a large eggplant become supple when grilled, so you can roll them around a ricotta filling as if you were making cannelloni from pasta squares. Blanketed with a homemade fresh-tomato sauce and baked until bubbly and a little crusty around the edges, the fork-tender bundles of stuffed eggplant are the ultimate Italian comfort food.

1   Slice off the eggplants' green cap, then cut each eggplant lengthwise into slices about ⅓ inch thick. Discard the first and last slices, which are mostly skin. You should get at least six large slices from each eggplant. Sprinkle them generously on both sides with salt, then set the slices on a rack and let stand for 30 minutes. Moisture will bead on the surface.

2   Prepare a moderate charcoal fire or preheat a gas grill to medium (375°F). Pat the eggplant slices dry with paper towels, then brush on both sides with the olive oil. Place the slices directly over the coals or gas flame and cook, turning once, until they are nicely marked by the grill and pliable, about 3 minutes per side. They do not need to be fully cooked as they will cook further in the oven. Set the slices aside on a tray to cool.

3 To make the tomato sauce, heat the olive oil in a large skillet over moderate heat. Add the onion and garlic and sauté until the onion is soft and beginning to color, 5 to 10 minutes. Add the tomatoes and cook, stirring often, until they soften and collapse into a sauce, about 10 minutes, depending on ripeness.

4 Remove from the heat, and pass the mixture through a food mill fitted with the fine disk. Return the puree to the skillet over moderate heat. Tear the basil leaves in half and add to the skillet along with the oregano (rubbing it between your fingers as you do), the hot pepper flakes, and salt to taste. Simmer gently, stirring occasionally, until the sauce is thick and tasty. Set aside.

5 To make the ricotta filling, put the ricotta, pecorino, prosciutto, parsley, and garlic in a medium bowl. Stir until blended, then season to taste with salt and pepper. Stir in the egg.

6 Preheat the oven to 350°F. Choose a shallow baking dish large enough to hold all the eggplant rolls snugly in one layer. Spread ⅓ cup of the tomato sauce on the bottom of the dish.

7 Put a generous 2 tablespoons filling on each eggplant slice and spread it evenly. Carefully roll each slice like a jelly roll, and place the rolls, seam side down, in the baking dish. Top with the remaining tomato sauce, spreading it evenly. Sprinkle the pecorino evenly over the top.

8 Bake until lightly browned and bubbling, about 45 minutes. Cool for 20 minutes before serving.

Lamb Burgers

with Grilled Red Onions and Feta

SERVES 6

Lamb shoulder has sufficient internal marbling to make a juicy burger. When ground, it is the lamb equivalent of ground chuck. Grill the patties, then layer them on a soft bun with tomato, smoky onions, and crumbled feta to make a burger with a Middle Eastern accent. Sumac, a brick red spice sold at Middle Eastern markets, has an invigorating lemony tang that complements grilled meat.

1   Prepare a moderate charcoal fire for indirect grilling (page xi) or preheat a gas grill to medium (375° to 400°F), leaving one burner unlit.

2   Put the lamb in a large bowl. Add the oregano (crumbling it between your fingers as you add it), 2 teaspoons of salt, and hot pepper flakes, and season with black pepper. Work the seasonings in gently, then, with moistened hands, shape the meat into six patties each about ⅜ inch thick. They should be a little wider than your hamburger buns, as they will shrink in diameter when cooked.

3   From opposing directions, insert two toothpicks horizontally into each red onion slice; the toothpicks will hold the onion layers together on the grill. Brush the onion slices on both sides with some of the olive oil and season with salt and pepper.

Ingredients

2 pounds freshly ground lamb shoulder

1 tablespoon plus 1 teaspoon dried oregano

Kosher or sea salt and freshly ground black pepper

½ teaspoon hot red pepper flakes

6 red onion slices, ½ inch thick

1 tablespoon extra virgin olive oil

⅓ pound Greek, French, Bulgarian, or Israeli feta cheese, at room temperature, crumbled

6 hamburger buns, split

Ground sumac (optional)

2 tomatoes, thinly sliced

Feta cheese (optional)

4 Grill the onion slices first: Place them directly over the coals or gas flame and cover the grill. Cook, turning once, until nicely colored on both sides, about 5 minutes, then move to indirect heat until they are softened but not limp, about 5 minutes longer. Keep warm while you grill the burgers.

5 Grill the burgers directly over the coals or gas flame—lid off on a charcoal grill, lid on for a gas grill. Cook until they are done to your taste, which you can best determine by touch. A rare burger feels soft, with no spring back. A medium burger will offer some resistance to the touch, but will not feel firm. A well-done burger will be firm to the touch. Cooking time depends on the heat of your fire, but a medium burger will take about 10 minutes. A couple of minutes before the burgers are done, top with the feta, dividing it evenly, and toast the bun halves on the grill, cut side down.

6 To assemble the burgers, place the bottom halves of the buns, cut side up, on individual plates. Sprinkle generously with sumac. Top with tomato slices and sprinkle with salt. Remove the toothpicks from the onion slices and place on top of the tomato. Top the onion with a burger, sprinkle with feta cheese and sumac, then cover with the top half of the bun. Serve immediately.

Ingredients

12 large cloves garlic

3 tablespoons chopped fresh rosemary, or 1 tablespoon dried

1 tablespoon coarse salt

½ teaspoon freshly ground black pepper

1 (4- to 6-pound) leg of lamb, boned and butterflied (see Tip, right)

2 large lemons

3 or 4 sprigs rosemary, for garnish

Grilled Butterflied
Leg of Lamb

SERVES 8

For entertaining, almost nothing beats a butterflied leg of lamb. Its preparation is simpler than simple, and the cooking time is short. Plus, great meals can be planned around the leftovers, including a Greek-style sandwich of sliced lamb, crumbled feta, sliced cucumbers, and tomatoes, or a salad of bulgur, chopped romaine, lemon juice, olive oil, and garlic topped with sliced lamb. Serve the grilled lamb with Marinated Grilled Zucchini (page 54).

1 In a large, heavy mortar, combine the garlic, rosemary, salt, and pepper. Pound the garlic to a paste, stirring it with the other ingredients until combined. Alternatively, grate or press the garlic onto a plate and use a fork to mash the other ingredients into the garlic until blended.

2 Place the lamb on a rimmed sheet pan or in a large baking dish. With your fingertips, rub half of the garlic paste on the surface of the lamb, spreading it evenly into all of the crevices. Turn the lamb over and repeat on the other side.

3 Thinly slice and seed one lemon and spread the slices on the lamb. Halve the remaining lemon and squeeze the juice over the surface of the lamb. Cover the pan with plastic wrap and refrigerate for at least 2 hours or as long as overnight. Remove the lamb from the refrigerator 1 hour before grilling or broiling.

4 Prepare a moderate charcoal fire or preheat a gas grill to medium (375°F). Scrape the lemon slices off the lamb and reserve. Grill the lamb for 10 to 12 minutes per side for the thickest piece and for 8 minutes per side for the thinner pieces, or until an instant-read thermometer registers 140°F for medium-rare. Toward the end of the grilling time, arrange the lemon slices on the grill and heat just until golden. Reserve the lemon slices for garnishing the lamb.

5 Alternatively, the lamb can be broiled: Position an oven rack in the top of the oven so that the top of the broiler pan will be about 5 inches from the heat source, and preheat the broiler. Place the lamb on a broiler pan and broil using the same time and internal temperature guidelines used for grilling. Toward the end of the broiling time, place the lemon slices on the surface of the lamb and broil just until golden. Reserve the lemon for garnishing the lamb.

6 Transfer the meat to a wooden board and let rest for 5 to 10 minutes. Carve the meat across the grain into thin slices. Arrange the slices on a warmed serving platter in neat overlapping rows. Pour the meat juices and the seasonings that have accumulated on the board into a small saucepan, reheat briefly, and pour over the meat slices. Garnish with rosemary sprigs and the grilled or broiled lemon slices and serve at once.

TIP: Leg of Lamb, Anatomically Speaking
Because a butterflied leg of lamb is a rather free-form mass of muscle and flesh, and thus thicker in some spots than others, there is no way to grill or broil it in one piece successfully. The solution is to divide the lamb into pieces following the anatomy of the leg. To do this, position the lamb, smooth side down, on a cutting board and divide it following the natural separations. Then turn the pieces of lamb over and make sure the butcher has trimmed off all but a thin layer of fat. If not, use a thin, sharp knife or a boning knife to trim away any excess.

Lemon-Caper Butter

½ cup unsalted butter (1 stick), softened

2 tablespoons capers, preferably salt packed, rinsed and finely minced

2 teaspoons grated lemon zest

2 tablespoons minced fresh Italian parsley

Kosher or sea salt

1 pound sea scallops

Kosher or sea salt and freshly ground black pepper

1 tablespoon unsalted butter, melted

3 bunches (12 to 14 ounces each) spinach, thick stems removed

4 lemon wedges

Grilled Scallops with Wilted Spinach

and Lemon-Caper Butter

SERVES 4

In just a few moments on the stove, a potful of rough fresh spinach leaves wilts down into a silky bed for grilled scallops. A composed butter enlivened with capers and lemon zest creates a simple sauce as it melts on the hot greens and shellfish. Be sure to warm the dinner plates for a few minutes in a low oven to keep the food hot. Both the spinach and the scallops cool off quickly otherwise.

1 Prepare a moderate charcoal fire or preheat a gas grill to medium (375°F). To make the lemon-caper butter, put the butter, capers, lemon zest, and parsley in a bowl and stir with a wooden spoon until smooth. Season to taste with salt.

2 Remove the "foot" or small muscle on the side of each scallop. Halve the scallops horizontally, or slice them in thirds if they are jumbo scallops, so the slices are no more than ½ inch thick. Season all over with salt and pepper and brush with the melted butter.

3 Put the spinach in a large pot with just the washing water clinging to the leaves. Cover and cook over moderate heat, stirring with tongs once or twice, until the spinach is barely wilted, about 3 minutes. Drain in a sieve or colander. Do not

press on the leaves or squeeze them to extract more liquid; you want to leave them fairly moist. Return them to the same pot and add half of the lemon-caper butter. Toss with tongs over low heat so that the butter melts and coats the spinach. Taste for salt. Keep the spinach warm while you grill the scallops.

4   Grill the scallops directly over the coals or gas flame, turning once, until they are nicely marked by the grill and no longer translucent, about 5 minutes total.

5   Divide the spinach among warmed dinner plates. Arrange the scallops on top, and immediately slather the scallops with the remaining butter. The butter will melt from the heat of the shellfish. Garnish each serving with a lemon wedge and serve immediately.

Ingredients

Peperonata

3 tablespoons extra virgin olive oil

½ large red onion, thinly sliced

2 cloves garlic, minced

1 cup grated plum (Roma type) tomato (see note)

2 large bell peppers, 1 red and 1 gold, seeds removed and cut lengthwise into ¼-inch-wide strips

Kosher or sea salt

Generous pinch of hot red pepper flakes

1½ tablespoons capers, preferably salt packed, rinsed

Red or white wine vinegar

12 fresh basil leaves

4 swordfish steaks, about 6 ounces each and ½ inch thick

Extra virgin olive oil

Kosher or sea salt

1 teaspoon fennel seed, crushed in a mortar or spice grinder

• • • • • • • • • • • • • • • • • • • •

NOTE: To grate plum (Roma type) tomatoes, cut the tomatoes in half lengthwise. Discard the seeds if the recipe directs. Grate the tomato flesh on the coarse holes of a box grater until only the tomato skin remains in your hand. Discard the skin.

Grilled Swordfish
with Peperonata

SERVES 4

In Italy, *peperonata*—braised peppers with tomato and onion—is typically served as an antipasto or side dish, but it makes a superb fish topping. Substitute tuna, halibut, or cod for the swordfish, if you prefer. Swordfish should be sliced thin and cooked quickly for maximum juiciness. If your merchant has already sliced it into thick steaks, ask to have it halved horizontally, or do it at home yourself with a long, thin knife.

1 To make the *peperonata*, heat 2 tablespoons of the olive oil in a large skillet over moderately low heat. Add the onion and garlic and sauté until the onion is soft, about 5 minutes. Add the tomato and simmer until it loses its raw taste, about 5 minutes. Add the bell peppers and season with salt and hot pepper flakes. Cover and simmer gently until the peppers are tender, about 25 minutes. Add a tablespoon or two of water if the mixture looks dry, or uncover the skillet at the end of cooking to evaporate moisture if the mixture is too juicy. The juices should be concentrated, not runny. Stir in the capers and a splash of vinegar to brighten the flavor, then taste for salt. Set aside to cool until just warm, not hot. Stir in the basil, torn into smaller pieces.

2 While the *peperonata* is cooking, prepare a moderate charcoal fire or preheat a gas grill to medium (375°F). When the *peperonata* has been set aside to cool, brush the fish generously on both sides with olive oil, then season on both sides with salt and fennel seed. Grill directly over the coals or gas flame, turning once, until the fish is white throughout but still juicy, 2 to 3 minutes per side.

3 Transfer the swordfish to a serving platter. Top each steak with some of the warm *peperonata*, mounding it attractively. Serve immediately.

Brine

1 quart lukewarm water

2½ tablespoons kosher or sea salt

6 thyme sprigs

2 large cloves garlic, sliced

1 pork tenderloin, 1 pound

Yogurt Sauce

1½ cups plain yogurt, preferably whole milk

1 large clove garlic, finely minced

¼ cup finely chopped fresh dill

Kosher or sea salt

1 large red onion

1 large red or gold bell pepper, seeded and cut into 1-inch squares

1 large green bell pepper, seeded and cut into 1-inch squares

¼ cup extra virgin olive oil

3 cloves garlic, thickly sliced

1 tablespoon minced fresh rosemary

½ teaspoon hot red pepper flakes

¾ teaspoon kosher or sea salt

24 cubes focaccia (1-inch cubes)

Spicy Pork, Focaccia, and Sweet Pepper Kebabs

SERVES 6

Any type of sweet pepper works in this recipe, from meaty bells and pimientos to elongated frying peppers, like *Corno di Toro* and Gypsy. The thin-walled frying peppers are an especially good choice because they cook through in about the same time as the pork. Bell peppers, with their thick walls, remain a little firmer when the pork is done, but they are still tasty. Brining the lean pork tenderloin helps to keep it moist.

1 To make the brine, put the lukewarm water and salt in a bowl and stir together until the salt dissolves and the water becomes clear. Add the thyme sprigs and garlic. Cool to room temperature. Put the pork tenderloin in a container that holds it snugly. Add the brine. It should cover the pork. Cover with plastic wrap. Alternatively, you can put the pork and its brine in a 1-gallon heavy-duty resealable food storage bag. Refrigerate for 8 to 12 hours. One hour before cooking, remove the pork from the brine and pat dry. Cut it into twenty-four roughly uniform chunks.

2 Prepare a moderate charcoal fire for indirect grilling (page xi) or preheat a gas grill to medium (375°F), leaving one of the burners unlit. To make the yogurt sauce, in a bowl, whisk together the yogurt, garlic, and dill. Season to taste with salt.

3 Halve the onion through the stem end, then cut into roughly 1-inch cubes. Separate the onion layers. In a large bowl, combine the pork, onion, bell peppers, olive oil, garlic, rosemary, hot pepper flakes, and salt. Toss to coat the meat and vegetables with the seasonings. Add the focaccia and toss again.

4 Thread the focaccia, pork, onion, and peppers onto metal or wooden skewers, alternating them attractively and using all the ingredients.

Put the skewers over indirect heat. Cover the grill and cook for about 4 minutes, then turn and cook until the pork feels medium-firm to the touch and the vegetables have softened slightly, 3 to 4 minutes longer. If necessary, put the skewers over direct heat for the final couple of minutes to char the ingredients lightly, but watch carefully to avoid burning the focaccia. Serve the kebabs immediately, passing the yogurt sauce separately.

Ingredients

Hickory Rib Rub

½ cup store-bought hickory-smoked salt or kosher salt

¼ cup garlic powder or granulated garlic

¼ cup onion powder

¼ cup chili powder

3 tablespoons sweet Hungarian paprika

3 tablespoons firmly packed light or dark brown sugar

3 tablespoons dry mustard

1½ tablespoons ground ginger

1½ tablespoons red pepper flakes

4 (1½-pound) slabs baby back ribs, back membrane removed

Hickory wood chips

1 (16-ounce) squeeze bottle clover or other amber honey

2 cups tomato-based barbecue sauce

Hickory-Grilled
Baby Back Ribs

SERVES 8

Baby back ribs take well to grilling for a sweet, smoky, spicy, and deliciously sticky finish. For a more tender result, remove the membrane on the underside of the ribs by detaching it with a sharp knife, then pulling it off with your fingers or needle-nose pliers.

1 To make the rub, combine all ingredients in a bowl. Sprinkle both sides of each slab with the rub.

2 Prepare a moderate charcoal fire (page ix) or preheat a gas grill to medium (375°F).

3 Grill the slabs for 15 minutes per side, turning every 5 minutes, or until slightly browned.

4 Transfer the ribs to a baking sheet. For a charcoal grill, lift up the grill grate, brush the coals to one side, and throw moistened wood chips directly on the coals. Replace the grill grate. For a gas grill, turn off a burner, enclose the wood chips in a metal smoker box or an aluminum foil packet with holes poked in the top, and place the box or packet on the grill grate over the heat source.

5 When you see the first wisp of wood smoke, place the slabs on the indirect side, using a rib rack if you like. Cover and grill, turning or repositioning the ribs every 10 to 15 minutes, for 30 minutes longer, or until the meat begins to pull back from the ends of the bone about ½ inch.

6 Squeeze the honey on both sides of the ribs and brush to cover the meat. Then brush on the barbecue sauce. Cover and grill for another 10 to 15 minutes, turning several times, until the sauce on the ribs has caramelized. Serve one-half slab per person.

Grilled Sausages with Baby Turnips

and Turnip Greens

The best turnips for this preparation are the small white Tokyo turnips, so thin skinned that they don't need to be peeled. The more familiar purple-topped white globe turnips will need peeling unless they are very young.

1 Prepare a hot charcoal fire or preheat a gas grill to high (450° to 500°F).

2 Cut the turnips away from their greens, leaving no stem attached. Remove the stems from the greens but not the ribs at the center of each leaf. You should have about 1 pound of trimmed turnip greens. Peel the turnips if the skin feels thick; otherwise, leave them unpeeled. Cut the turnips in half if they are smaller than a golf ball; quarter them if they are larger.

3 Bring a large pot of salted water to a boil over high heat. Add the turnip greens and boil until they are tender, 3 to 5 minutes, depending on their size and age. Drain in a sieve or colander and immediately run under cold running water until cool. Drain again and squeeze to remove excess moisture. Chop coarsely.

Ingredients

2 to 2½ pounds turnips (about 10 golf ball–size turnips with greens attached)

¼ cup extra virgin olive oil

1 small dried red chile, broken in half

Kosher or sea salt

2 large cloves garlic, minced

4 fresh sausages (such as hot or sweet Italian), about 6 ounces each

Hot pepper vinegar (optional)

4   Heat the olive oil in a large skillet over
    moderate heat. Add the turnips and chile,
    season with salt, and toss to coat with the
    oil. Cover and reduce the heat to moderately
    low. Cook until the turnips are lightly browned
    in spots on the cut sides and almost tender
    when pierced, about 5 minutes. Add the
    garlic and cook, uncovered, stirring, for 1
    minute to release its fragrance. Add the
    chopped greens and cook, stirring, until they
    are hot throughout and coated with oil. Taste
    and adjust the seasoning. Keep warm while
    you grill the sausages.

5   Grill the sausages directly over the coals or
    gas flame, turning often and moving them as
    necessary to prevent flare-ups. They are done
    when the internal temperature registers 145°
    to 150°F on an instant-read thermometer.

6   Put the sausages on a platter and surround
    them with the greens and turnips, or pass
    the vegetables separately. Serve immediately.
    Offer hot pepper vinegar for the greens.

Grilled
Five-Spice Chicken

SERVES 4

Popular at Vietnamese restaurants, this dish is easy to replicate at home. You can use the same marinade on chicken parts, but a whole butterflied chicken is dramatic and less trouble to maneuver on a grill. Because the marinade contains sugar, the chicken skin will char easily if placed directly over the coals or gas flame, so cook the bird over indirect heat the entire time. The exterior will still develop a honey brown gloss thanks to the soy sauce and five-spice powder.

1   To butterfly the chicken, you need to remove the backbone. You can do this with poultry shears or a chef's knife. If using poultry shears, turn the chicken, breast side down, on a cutting board and cut from the neck to the tail along both sides of the backbone to release it. If using a chef's knife, turn the chicken, breast side up, on a cutting board. Insert the chef's knife into the body cavity and cut along both sides of the backbone to release it. With the breast side up, press on the breastbone with the heel of your hand to flatten the bird. Cut off the wing tips and discard.

2   To make the marinade, put the garlic, shallot, lemongrass, ginger, and sugar in a food processor and pulse until very finely chopped. With the motor running, add the soy sauce through the feed tube and puree until the paste is as fine as possible. Transfer to a bowl and whisk in the fish sauce, five-spice powder, and pepper.

Ingredients

1 whole chicken, 3½ to 4 pounds

Marinade

6 cloves garlic, thinly sliced

1 large shallot, coarsely chopped

2 tablespoons minced lemongrass

1 tablespoon peeled and minced fresh ginger

1 tablespoon plus 1 teaspoon light brown sugar

¼ cup soy sauce

¼ cup fish sauce (see note, page 23)

1 teaspoon five-spice powder

½ teaspoon freshly ground black pepper

3 Place the flattened chicken in a large baking dish, pour the marinade over it, and turn the bird to coat on both sides. Cover with plastic wrap and refrigerate. Alternatively, you can put the chicken and its marinade in a 1-gallon heavy-duty resealable food storage bag and refrigerate. Marinate for 6 to 8 hours.

4 Remove the chicken from the refrigerator about 1 hour before you plan to grill. Prepare a moderate charcoal fire for indirect grilling (page xi) or preheat a gas grill to medium (375°F), leaving one burner unlit for indirect grilling.

5 Remove the chicken from the marinade, reserving the marinade. Brush the skin side of the chicken with some of the marinade. Place the chicken, skin side down, over indirect heat. Cover the grill and cook until the skin is richly browned and crisp, 15 to 20 minutes. Brush the flesh side of the chicken with the remaining marinade, then turn the chicken, skin side up, cover the grill, and continue grilling over indirect heat until the juices run clear when a thigh is pierced, or an instant-read thermometer inserted in the thickest part of the thigh away from the bone registers 165°F, about 15 minutes longer. Let rest for 10 minutes before carving into serving pieces.

Ingredients

1 flank steak, about 1½ pounds

¼ cup extra virgin olive oil

¼ cup dry red wine

4 cloves garlic, thinly sliced

1 tablespoon Dijon mustard

1 tablespoon minced fresh
   rosemary

Creamed Spinach

2 pounds spinach, thick stems
   removed

1½ tablespoons unsalted butter

1½ tablespoons unbleached all-
   purpose flour

¾ cup whole milk

¼ cup heavy cream

Whole nutmeg, for grating

Kosher or sea salt and freshly
   ground black pepper

2 teaspoons Pernod or pastis

Grilled Flank Steak
with Old-Fashioned Creamed Spinach

SERVES 4

A classic steak-house favorite, creamed spinach blossoms with a
dash of an anise-scented spirit, such as Pernod or pastis. Simmered
in cream-enriched béchamel, it is rich and indulgent but worth every
calorie.

1 Place the flank steak flat in a nonreactive container. In a small
bowl, whisk together the olive oil, wine, garlic, mustard, and
rosemary. Pour this marinade over the meat and turn the meat
to distribute the seasonings evenly. Cover with plastic wrap and
refrigerate for 8 hours, turning the meat once halfway through.

2 Remove the meat from the refrigerator about 1 hour before you
plan to grill it. Prepare a moderate charcoal fire or preheat a
gas grill to medium (375°F).

3 To make the creamed spinach, bring a large pot of salted water
to a boil over high heat. Add the spinach, pushing it down
into the water with tongs. As soon as it wilts—less than 30
seconds—drain in a sieve or colander and immediately run
under cold running water until cool. Drain again and squeeze to
remove excess moisture. Chop finely.

4 Melt the butter in a medium saucepan over moderately low
heat. Add the flour and whisk until well blended and bubbling,

about 1 minute. Whisk in the milk and cream and bring to a simmer. Adjust the heat to maintain a gentle simmer and cook, whisking often, for about 5 minutes to eliminate the raw flour taste.

5   Add the spinach and season with several scrapings of nutmeg and salt and pepper. Gently simmer the spinach for about 10 minutes to blend the flavors, stirring often with a wooden spoon. Stir in the Pernod and reduce the heat to low. Keep warm while you grill the steak.

6   Remove the steak from the marinade and season it on both sides with salt and pepper. Grill directly over the coals or gas flame, turning once, for about 5 minutes per side for rare to medium-rare. Because it is so lean, flank steak is best if not cooked beyond medium-rare. Let the meat rest for 10 minutes before slicing.

7   To slice the steak, hold a chef's knife at an angle of about 30 degrees to the cutting board to make broad, wide slices. Serve with the creamed spinach on the side.

Ingredients

Oyster Sauce

1 large clove garlic, minced

1 inch fresh ginger, grated

2 tablespoons chicken broth

1 tablespoons oyster sauce

1½ teaspoons soy sauce

1 teaspoon toasted sesame oil

1 teaspoon Chinese rice wine or
dry sherry

1 tablespoon peanut oil

1 pound boneless, skinless
chicken breast or thigh, cut into
2-inch pieces

1 pound baby bok choy, cut in half
lengthwise

8 ounces button mushrooms,
sliced

½ fresh red chile, seeded and
sliced

Steamed rice for serving

Stir-Grilled Chicken, Mushrooms, and Baby Bok Choy
in Oyster Sauce

SERVES 4

With steamed rice, this stir-grilled dish makes a wonderful meal. Stir-grilling involves marinating foods, then stirring them with wooden paddles or spoons as they cook in a grill wok to a caramelized finish.

1   To make the sauce, combine the garlic, ginger, chicken broth, oyster sauce, soy sauce, sesame oil, rice wine, and peanut oil in a large bowl. Add the chicken, bok choy, mushrooms, and chile and toss to blend. Cover and let marinate in the refrigerator for 30 minutes.

2   Prepare a very hot charcoal fire or preheat a gas grill to high (450° to 500°F). Oil the inside of a grill wok.

3   Place the grill wok on the grill grate. Add the chicken mixture to the grill wok. Cover the grill and let cook for 2 minutes. Stir the mixture with wooden paddles or a long-handled wooden spoon, cover, and cook again for 2 minutes. At 2-minute intervals, stir, cover, and cook for 10 more minutes or until the chicken is opaque and firm.

4   Transfer the stir-grilled food to a serving bowl. Serve atop steamed rice.

4 bone-in ribeye steaks (each
    about 18 ounces), about 1-inch
    thick

Olive oil for brushing

Salt and pepper

⅓ cup moistened wood chips, such
    as hickory or mesquite

Chipotle Butter (page 33)

....

Wood-Grilled

Cowboy Ribeye with Chipotle Butter

SERVES 4

A cowboy ribeye is a thick, bone-in steak that deserves special grilling techniques. Adding mesquite chips to the fire infuses the steak with savory wood smoke. Searing the steak first over direct heat, then transferring it to the indirect side, helps the steak grill perfectly. Chipotle Butter adds a final taste of the American West.

1 Prepare a very hot charcoal fire for indirect grilling (page xi) or preheat a gas grill to high (450° to 500°F), leaving one of the burners unlit.

2 Brush the steaks on both sides with olive oil and season to taste.

3 If using a charcoal grill, throw moistened wood chips directly on the coals right before you want to grill. If using a gas grill, enclose the wood chips or pellets in a metal smoker box or an aluminum foil packet with holes poked in the top; place the box or packet on the grill grate over the heat source.

4 When you see the first wisp of wood smoke, place the steaks on the hot side, cover the grill, and cook for 3 to 4 minutes per side, or until the steaks have good grill marks. Transfer the steaks to the indirect side, close the lid, and continue grilling for

2 to 3 minutes, turning once (135° to 140°F for medium rare; 145° to 150°F for medium). Let the steaks rest for 5 minutes before serving.

5 Serve a dollop of Chipotle Butter on each steak.

Ingredients

Gorgonzola Sauce

¼ cup crumbled Gorgonzola or other blue cheese

1 large clove garlic, minced

¼ cup olive oil

2 tablespoons balsamic vinegar

Salt and pepper

1 (1½-pound) boneless sirloin steak, cut 2 inches thick

3 tablespoons olive oil

4 cups baby arugula or spinach leaves (or other leafy lettuce of your choice)

1 cup cherry or currant tomatoes

1 cup thinly sliced red onion

Lemon wedges for garnish

Black and Blue Sirloin on a Bed of Arugula
with Gorgonzola Sauce

SERVES 8; MAKES ⅔ CUP SAUCE

A thick steak offers many rewards for the griller. It's more foolproof than a thinner steak, and it goes farther to feed friends and family—especially when sliced and served over greens, then drizzled with a savory sauce. This steak will have a charred exterior and a rare or "blue" center. Those who prefer a medium doneness can grill it 2 to 3 minutes longer.

1 To make the sauce, whisk the Gorgonzola, garlic, olive oil, and balsamic vinegar, together in a small bowl. Season to taste. If you wish, funnel the sauce into a squeeze bottle, or simply leave in the bowl and set aside.

2 Prepare a very hot charcoal fire (page ix) or preheat a gas grill to high (450° to 500°F). Brush the steaks on both sides with olive oil and season to taste.

3 Place the steaks on the grill grate and grill, uncovered, for 8 minutes, turning once (130° for rare; 135° to 140°F for medium rare). Remove the steak from the grill and let it rest for 5 minutes.

4 Arrange the greens, tomatoes, and onion slices on a serving platter. Slice the steak thinly and place the slices on top of the greens. Squeeze or drizzle the sauce over the steak and greens and garnish with lemon wedges.

Ingredients

Fresh Tomato Relish

1 pint yellow and red cherry tomatoes, halved

1 cup baby greens or arugula

2 tablespoons finely chopped red onion

1 jalapeño pepper, seeded and diced

2 garlic cloves, minced

¼ cup finely minced Italian parsley

2 tablespoons extra-virgin olive oil

2 tablespoons fresh lime juice

Fine kosher or sea salt and freshly ground black pepper

⅓ cup moistened wood chips, such as hickory or mesquite

1 pound ground chuck, formed into four 1-inch-thick patties

1 large red onion, peeled and cut into ½-inch-thick slices

1 small wheel (8 ounces) baby Brie

Olive oil for brushing

Fine kosher or sea salt and freshly ground black pepper

Seeded hamburger buns, kaiser rolls, or *ciabattini*, sliced in half

Wood-Grilled

Brie Burgers with Grilled Onions and Fresh Tomato Relish

SERVES 4; MAKES 4 CUPS RELISH

This decadent version of a traditional cheeseburger has style as well as great flavor. Adding wood to the fire—wood grilling—provides more of a smoky taste. Grilling a wheel of baby Brie is easy. It just needs to be turned once as soon as the cheese starts to ooze out of the rind. Once it has started to ooze on both sides, it should be taken off the grill. The relish is vegetable and salad rolled into one.

1 To make the relish, combine all the relish ingredients in a bowl. Cover and refrigerate until ready to serve.

2 Prepare a very hot charcoal fire or preheat a gas grill to high (450° to 500°F). If using a charcoal grill, throw moistened wood chips directly on the coals right before you want to grill. If using a gas grill, enclose the wood chips or pellets in a metal smoker box or an aluminum foil packet with holes poked in the top; place the box or packet on the grill grate over the heat source.

3 Oil a perforated grill rack and place on the grill.

4 Brush the red onion slices and the Brie with olive oil on both sides, and season to taste.

5 When you see the first wisp of wood smoke, place the onions and baby Brie on the prepared perforated grill rack and the burgers on the grill grate. Cover the grill. Grill the onions and Brie, turning once, for 7 to 8 minutes. Grill the burgers, turning once, for 7 minutes for medium. Grill the cut sides of the buns or rolls for 1 minute, or until just warmed and slightly browned.

6 To serve, place each burger on a bottom bun and top with the grilled onions. Cut the Brie into four wedges and place a wedge on top of each burger. Replace the top bun on each burger. Serve with the relish on the side.

Ingredients

Fiesta Slaw

1 cup finely shredded green
   cabbage

1 cup thinly sliced radishes

½ cup finely chopped green onion

2 tablespoons finely chopped fresh
   cilantro

3 tablespoons fresh orange juice

2 tablespoons fresh lime juice

2 tablespoons vegetable oil

Salt and pepper

1 pound skinless mahimahi,
   pompano, yellow snapper,
   halibut, or cod fillet, about
   ¾ inch thick

Olive oil

8 flour tortillas, about 6 inches in
   diameter, warmed

1 cup *crema* or sour cream

Grilled Baja Fish Tacos
with Fiesta Slaw

SERVES 4

Fish tacos from Baja California combine the tang of fresh lime juice
with the tenderness of fresh fish and the flavor of the grill. The general
rules for grilling fish include brushing the fish with oil, using a hot
fire, and grilling the fish for 10 minutes total per inch of thickness
(measured in the thickest part). That means these ¾-inch fish fillets
will be done in 7 to 8 minutes.

1 To make the slaw, combine the cabbage, radishes, green onion,
   and cilantro in a large bowl. In a small bowl, whisk the juices
   and oil together, then season to taste. Pour over the vegetables
   and toss to blend.

2 Prepare a very hot charcoal fire or preheat a gas grill to high
   (450° to 500°F).

3 Brush the fish with oil and season to taste.

4 Grill the fish for 3 to 4 minutes per side, using a fish spatula
   to turn it once. The fish is done when it begins to flake when
   tested with the tip of a small knife in the thickest part.

5 Transfer the fish to a serving platter. Top with the slaw. Pass the
   warm tortillas and *crema* at the table.

6 To serve, place a spoonful of fish and slaw in the center of a
   warm flour tortilla and dollop with *crema*.

Desserts

Grilled Pound Cake

with Strawberry-Rhubarb Sauce

SERVES 8

Many fans of pound cake know that toasting it heightens the cake's buttery flavor. Grilling works the same magic, so when you have the grill going for a summer dinner, why not grill dessert, too? Be sure to brush the grill rack clean first.

1   To make the cake, preheat the oven to 325°F. Lightly grease a 9 by 5 by 3-inch loaf pan with butter. Coat the bottom and sides with flour and shake out the excess.

2   Sift together the flour, salt, and baking powder into a medium bowl.

3   In the bowl of a stand mixer fitted with the paddle, or in a large bowl with a handheld mixer, cream the butter on medium speed until smooth. Add the sugar gradually, beating constantly until the mixture is light and fluffy. Beat in the eggs, one at a time, beating well after each addition and scraping down the sides of the bowl once or twice, then beat in the lemon zest and poppy seeds. On low speed, add the dry ingredients gradually, beating just until blended. Transfer the batter to the prepared pan, spreading it evenly.

Ingredients

Pound Cake

1 cup (2 sticks) unsalted butter, softened, plus more for preparing the pan

2 cups sifted unbleached all-purpose flour, plus more for preparing the pan

½ teaspoon kosher or sea salt

¼ teaspoon baking powder

1½ cups sugar

5 large eggs, at room temperature

1 tablespoon freshly grated lemon zest

1 tablespoon poppy seeds

Strawberry-Rhubarb Sauce

1 pint strawberries, cored and quartered lengthwise

½ pound rhubarb, trimmed and cut crosswise into ½-inch pieces

2 tablespoons fresh orange juice

6 to 8 tablespoons sugar

Vanilla ice cream

4   Bake until the cake is firm to the touch and beginning to pull away from the sides of the pan, about 1¼ hours. A cake tester inserted in the middle should come out clean. Cool the cake in the pan on a rack for 15 minutes, then invert onto a rack. Invert again so the top is up and finish cooling on the rack.

5   To make the strawberry-rhubarb sauce, put the berries, rhubarb, orange juice, and 6 tablespoons sugar in a medium saucepan. Set over moderate heat and heat, stirring until the sugar dissolves. Cover, adjust the heat to maintain a gentle simmer, and cook, stirring occasionally, until the fruit softens and forms a sauce, about 10 minutes. Keep a close eye on the saucepan, reducing the heat if the mixture threatens to bubble over. Cool slightly, then taste and add more sugar if desired. Transfer to a bowl, cover, and chill thoroughly.

6   Prepare a moderately hot charcoal fire or preheat a gas grill to medium-high (375° to 400°F). Cut the ends off the cake, then cut the cake into 8 equal slices. Grill directly over the coals or gas flame, turning once, until lightly toasted on both sides, about 2 minutes per side.

7   Put about ⅓ cup of the sauce on each dessert plate. Top with a slice of toasted cake and a scoop of ice cream. Serve immediately.

Grilled Nectarines

with Vanilla Ice Cream and Crushed Amaretti

Ingredients

3 nectarines, halved and pitted

1 tablespoon unsalted butter, melted

Vanilla ice cream

6 heaping tablespoons coarsely crushed amaretti

SERVES 6

If you've never grilled nectarines or other stone fruits (such as peaches, apricots, and plums), you are in for a treat. The direct heat caramelizes the surface, softens the flesh, and releases the sweet juices; with a scoop of ice cream snuggled up against the warm fruit, you have a luscious dessert. Crushed amaretti, the almond-flavored Italian cookies, add a crunchy contrast. To crush them easily, put them in a heavy plastic bag and smash with a rolling pin.

1 Prepare a moderate charcoal fire or preheat a gas grill to medium (375°F).

2 Brush the nectarine halves on both sides with the melted butter. Place the nectarines, cut side down, on the grill directly over the coals or gas flame. Cover the grill and cook until the nectarines are hot throughout, lightly caramelized on the surface, and slightly softened, 5 to 10 minutes. If they char too much before they soften, move them away from the coals or flame to finish cooking.

3 Put a nectarine half in each compote dish or stemmed glass. Top each nectarine half with a scoop of ice cream and a heaping tablespoon of crushed amaretti. Serve immediately.

Ingredients

Honeyed Crème Fraîche

1 cup heavy cream

1 cup sour cream

¼ cup honey

8 (12-inch) bamboo, metal, or wire skewers, or 8 kebab baskets

2 large, ripe carambola or star fruit, or 1 large pineapple, cut into 1-inch slices

16 fresh lychees, shelled and seeded, or whole kumquats

1 mango or papaya, peeled, pitted and cut into 2-inch chunks

4 limes, quartered

. . . .

Tropical Fruit Kebabs
with Honeyed Crème Fraîche

SERVES 8

A mix of unusual tropical fruits—star-shaped slices of star fruit, berry-like fresh lychees, chunks of mango or papaya—look great on skewers and taste delicious, but fresh pineapple is always your fallback position. Metal or flexible wire skewers or a kebab basket require no soaking beforehand as bamboo skewers do.

1 To make the crème fraîche, whisk the heavy cream and sour cream together and rest, covered, on a kitchen counter so it thickens in about 8 hours. Alternatively, you can buy prepared crème fraîche and stir in the honey. Set aside on the counter until needed.

2 If using bamboo skewers, soak the skewers in water for 30 minutes.

3 Assemble the skewers by threading the carambola slices lengthwise, piercing the skin of the fruit at one point of a star, going through the soft middle and through the point of a star on the other end. Alternate the other fruits, ending with a lime wedge.

4 Oil the grill grate. Prepare a moderate charcoal fire or preheat a gas grill to medium (375°F).

5   Grill the skewers, turning often, until the fruit is blistered, about 2 to 4 minutes per side.

6   Whisk the honey into the crème fraîche and transfer to a serving bowl. Serve the skewers on a serving platter. To eat, remove the fruit from the skewers, squeeze the grilled lime over all and enjoy with the crème fraîche.

Ingredients

Mexican Chocolate Ganache

2 (2.4- to 3.5-ounce) disks
  Mexican chocolate, from a
  package

1 cup heavy cream

1 large pineapple, peeled, cored,
  and cut into 1-inch-thick round
  slices

4 tablespoons unsalted butter,
  melted

1 pound cake, store-bought or
  homemade, sliced

....

Grilled Pineapple and Pound Cake

with Mexican Chocolate Ganache

SERVES 8

Mexican chocolate is a coarse blend of chocolate, sugar and sometimes cinnamon or ground chiles. It's meant for drinking, but it's also delicious in a more textured chocolate ganache, which tastes wonderful over grilled pineapple.

1 To make the ganache, combine the Mexican chocolate with heavy cream in a medium saucepan over low heat, whisking until the chocolate melts. Keep warm.

2 Prepare a very hot charcoal fire or preheat a gas grill to high (450° to 500°F).

3 Lightly brush the pineapple with the melted butter. Grill the pineapple slices for 3 to 4 minutes per side, or until they have good grill marks. Grill the pound cake slices for 1 to 2 minutes per side, or until they have good grill marks.

4 To serve, place the pineapple rings atop the pound cake slices. Spoon a little of the warm sauce over all.

Planked Papayas
with Fresh Lime Drizzle

SERVES 8

Shingled slices of fresh papaya, drizzled with fresh lime butter, look and taste wonderful planked. This method is also an easy way to make a fresh-tasting dessert.

1   Prepare a moderate charcoal fire for indirect grilling (page xi) or preheat a gas grill to medium (375°F), leaving one of the burners unlit.

2   In a bowl, combine the melted butter, brown sugar, lime zest and juice, and cayenne pepper.

3   Remove the planks from the water and pat dry. Divide the papaya between the planks, arranging them in one layer, shingle fashion. Brush the fruit with half of the lime mixture.

4   Place the planks over indirect heat. Cover the grill and cook for 10 to 15 minutes, or until the papaya is slightly burnished.

5   Serve the papaya right from the planks or transfer to a serving platter. Drizzle the fruit with the remaining sauce and garnish with lime wedges.

. . . .

Ingredients

2 cedar or oak grilling planks, soaked in water for at least 1 hour

4 tablespoons unsalted butter, melted

1 tablespoon light brown sugar

Zest and juice of 1 lime

1/8 teaspoon cayenne pepper or ground ancho chile

2 large, ripe papayas, peeled, seeded, pitted and cut into 2-inch slices

Fresh lime wedges for garnish

. . . .

Grilled
Banana Split

SERVES 4

The classic banana split gets a makeover in this recipe, using grilled bananas, fresh berries, and toasted almonds. Grilling bananas is easy, and this process also adds a touch of caramelization and a deepened flavor.

1 Prepare a very hot charcoal fire or preheat a gas grill to high (450° to 500°F).

2 Place the bananas, cut side down, directly over the hot fire and grill for about 2 to 3 minutes on the cut side only, until there are some grill marks.

3 Peel the bananas and cut in half again, and arrange in 4 shallow or sundae bowls. Put a scoop of ice cream in the center of each dish of bananas. Spoon the warm sauce over the top, garnish with berries, whipped cream and almonds and serve.

4 ripe yet firm bananas, halved lengthwise with the skin on

1 pint vanilla ice cream

Prepared chocolate sauce or Mexican Chocolate Ganache (page 110)

1 cup fresh blueberries

1 cup fresh sliced strawberries

Whipped cream and toasted sliced almonds, for garnish

Ingredients

Anise Ice Cream

2 cups half-and-half

1 teaspoon aniseed, lightly crushed in a mortar

6 large egg yolks

⅔ cup sugar

Pinch of kosher or sea salt

1 cup heavy cream

18 prune plums, halved and pitted

1½ to 2 tablespoons unsalted butter, melted

Grilled Prune Plums
with Anise ice Cream

SERVES 6

Prune plums are the small, intensely sweet varieties preferred by commercial dryers for making prunes. Sometimes known as French prunes or Italian prunes (depending on the variety), they are a late-summer treat that. Other plums tend to be too tart and watery to grill well, but you can pair this luscious ice cream with another grilled stone fruit, such as apricots, peaches, or nectarines.

1   To make the ice cream, combine the half-and-half and aniseed in a medium saucepan. Bring to a simmer over moderate heat. In a bowl, whisk the egg yolks, sugar, and salt until pale and thick. Add the contents of the saucepan gradually, whisking constantly, then return the mixture to the saucepan and set over moderate heat. Cook, stirring constantly with a wooden spoon, until the custard reaches 178°F on an instant-read thermometer. It will visibly thicken and coat the spoon. Do not let it boil or it will curdle.

2   Immediately transfer the custard to a bowl and cool for 15 minutes, then stir in the heavy cream. Cover the custard and refrigerate until well chilled.

3   Whisk the custard to distribute the aniseed evenly, then freeze in an ice-cream maker according to the manufacturer's directions. Transfer to a freezer container and freeze for at least 30 minutes to allow it to firm up before serving.

You will have about 1 quart of ice cream, which is more than you need for this recipe. The remainder will keep for up to 1 week.

4 Prepare a moderately hot charcoal fire or preheat a gas grill to medium-high (425°F). Thread the plums on wooden skewers. Brush with the melted butter. Grill, cut side down, directly over the coals or gas flame until the flesh begins to caramelize, 3 to 4 minutes, then turn and grill on the skin side until hot, 1 to 2 minutes.

5 Put a scoop of ice cream in each compote dish. Remove the hot plums from the skewers and divide them evenly among the dishes. Serve immediately.

Acknowledgments

Our kitchens have expanded. No longer is cooking confined to the four walls in our homes. We now can take advantage of the great outdoors all year long to extend the camaraderie that accompanies preparing a wonderful meal for family and friends.

So what could be more appropriate than our newest book, *Everyday Grilling: 50 Recipes from Appetizers to Desserts*, to punctuate the impromptu al fresco dining experience? It's all here in a great little treasure trove of recipes that make the most of your grill, every day of the week.

Most important, we thank our customers for demonstrating their excitement about grilling that inspired us to create this book to satiate their desires. Then it's Judith Fertig, Marie Simmons, and Janet Fletcher, who tempted their taste buds with the recipes, and Kirsty Melville, Jean Lucas, Tammie Barker, Ren-Wei Harn, Holly Ogden, Tim Lynch, John Carroll, and Carol Coe at Andrews McMeel, who tied the book with a bow in this wonderful little package. We thank Janis Donnaud for making sure all the ingredients were in place. Kudos to Gabe Hopkins and his assistant Kevin Porter, Sara Remington, Ben Fink, and the JohnsonRauhoff studio for making us salivate with the photos. They were ably assisted by Tina Stamos, Richard Garcia, and Kami Bremyer. At Sur La Table, Kate Dering, Sue Pippy, Linda Nangle, Claudia Saber, Felicia Chao, Bryan Haybeck, Mark Beard, Morgan McQuade, and Dave Bauer kept the many pieces from falling through the cracks.

So it's time to man your grilling station. We thank all of you for lighting the fire for *Everyday Grilling*!

Metric Conversions and Equivalents

Metric Conversion Formulas

TO CONVERT	MULTIPLY
Ounces to grams	Ounces by 28.35
Pounds to kilograms	Pounds by .454
Teaspoons to milliliters	Teaspoons by 4.93
Tablespoons to milliliters	Tablespoons by 14.79
Fluid ounces to milliliters	Fluid ounces by 29.57
Cups to milliliters	Cups by 236.59
Cups to liters	Cups by .236
Pints to liters	Pints by .473
Quarts to liters	Quarts by .946
Gallons to liters	Gallons by 3.785
Inches to centimeters	Inches by 2.54

Approximate Metric Equivalents

VOLUME

¼ teaspoon	1 milliliter
½ teaspoon	2.5 milliliters
¾ teaspoon	4 milliliters
1 teaspoon	5 milliliters
2 teaspoons	10 milliliters
1 tablespoon (½ fluid ounce)	15 milliliters
¼ cup	60 milliliters
⅓ cup	80 milliliters
½ cup (4 fluid ounces)	120 milliliters
⅔ cup	160 milliliters
¾ cup	180 milliliters
1 cup (8 fluid ounces)	240 milliliters
2 cups (1 pint)	460 milliliters
3 cups	700 milliliters
4 cups (1 quart)	.95 liter
1 quart plus ¼ cup	1 liter
4 quarts (1 gallon)	3.8 liters

WEIGHT

¼ ounce	7 grams
½ ounce	14 grams
¾ ounce	21 grams
1 ounce	28 grams
2 ounces	57 grams
3 ounces	85 grams
4 ounces (¼ pound)	113 grams
5 ounces	142 grams
6 ounces	170 grams
7 ounces	198 grams
8 ounces (½ pound)	227 grams
16 ounces (1 pound)	454 grams
35.25 ounces (2.2 pounds)	1 kilogram

LENGTH

¼ inch	6 millimeters
½ inch	1¼ centimeters
1 inch	2½ centimeters
2 inches	5 centimeters
6 inches	15¼ centimeters
12 inches (1 foot)	30 centimeters

Oven Temperatures
To convert Fahrenheit to Celsius, subtract 32 from Fahrenheit, multiply the result by 5, then divide by 9.

Description	Fahrenheit	Celsius	British Gas Mark
Very cool	200°	95°	0
Very cool	225°	110°	¼
Very cool	250°	120°	½
Cool	275°	135°	1
Cool	300°	150°	2
Warm	325°	165°	3
Moderate	350°	175°	4
Moderately hot	375°	190°	5
Fairly hot	400°	200°	6
Hot	425°	220°	7
Very hot	450°	230°	8
Very hot	475°	245°	9

Common Ingredients and Their Approximate Equivalents
1 cup uncooked rice = 225 grams
1 cup all-purpose flour = 140 grams
1 stick butter (4 ounces • ½ cup • 8 tablespoons) = 110 grams
1 cup butter (8 ounces • 2 sticks • 16 tablespoons) = 220 grams
1 cup brown sugar, firmly packed = 225 grams
1 cup granulated sugar = 200 grams

Information compiled from *Recipes into Type* by Joan Whitman and Dolores Simon (Newton, MA: Biscuit Books, 2000); *The New Food Lover's Companion* by Sharon Tyler Herbst (Hauppauge, NY: Barron's, 1995); and *Rosemary Brown's Big Kitchen Instruction Book* (Kansas City, MO: Andrews McMeel, 1998).

Index

Red Pepper Hummus, 26–27
relish, Fresh Tomato, 98–99
rhubarb, 105–6
rib chops, doneness chart, xiv
roaster, vertical, xv, xviii
romaine lettuce hearts, 10–12
rosemary, fresh, 74–75, 80–81, 90–91
rotisserie cooking method, xviii